Heritage of St. Louis

WRITERS
Helen I. Baldwin
Ruth M. Dockery
Nancy L. Garrett
S. Joseph Gore

PICTURE EDITOR
Helen H. Herminghaus

DESIGNER
Richard H. Brunell

ST. LOUIS PUBLIC SCHOOLS ⚜ ST. LOUIS, MISSOURI ⚜ 1964

James McDonnell ⚜ Annie Malone ⚜ John Berry Meachum ⚜ Stan Musial

John Peck ⚜ Joseph Pulitzer ⚜ John Queeny ⚜ Willam M. Reedy ⚜ Thomas Riddi

Dred Scott ⚜ Isaiah ⚜ Henry

William T. Sublet

George Vie Carl V

William Ashley ⚜ ⚜ Baptiste

Forest Park trolley

William Beaumont ⚜ James Beckwourth ⚜ Thomas Hart Benton ⚜ Susan Blow

August Busch ⚜ Robert Campbell ⚜ Joseph Charless ⚜ Auguste Chouteau ⚜ Pie

iv

ACKNOWLEDGEMENTS

Many persons and organizations contributed invaluable assistance in this work. The committee is most grateful to Miss Mary York and Mr. Philip Enzinger, who read the manuscript and made recommendations regarding it. Miss Dena Lange's contagious enthusiasm and knowledge of St. Louis history were a great help. Special appreciation must go to Miss Julia Davis and Dr. Reba Mosby, who contributed Negro historical references not otherwise available. Notable services were performed by Mr. J. Gilbert Princell and Miss Margaret Poetker, school photographers, and by Mrs. Gertrude B. Hoffsten, Manager of Radio Station KSLH.

The Social Studies Curriculum Committee, consisting of Mrs. Velma Appelbaum, Mrs. Daisy Bowden, Miss Dorothy Branding, and Mrs. Odessa Farrell, provided much needed help in incorporating the material of this book into the eighth grade social studies curriculum.

Valuable guidance was furnished by the members of the Project Advisory Board: Mrs. Elaine Afton, Miss Harriet Bick, Mrs. Virginia Brown, Dr. Earl G. Herminghaus, and Dr. Gerald Moeller of the public schools; Mrs. Robert Kelley and Mrs. Glen Moller of the White House Conference; Dr. Judson Shaplin, Director of the Graduate Institute of Education, Washington University; and Mr. George Brooks, Director of the Missouri Historical Society. A special debt is owed Mr. Brooks and Mrs. Ernest A. Stadler of the Missouri Historial Society, whose wise counsel and unfailing cooperation were of great help in this project.

Many of the pictures came from Mr. Leo January of the *St. Louis Globe-Democrat;* Mr. Roy King of the *St. Louis Post-Dispatch;* Mrs. Ruth K. Field of the Missouri Historical Society; the St. Louis Art Museum; and the Art Room of the St. Louis Public Library. Mrs. Dorothy Quest granted permission to use her copy of the painting of Pierre Laclede.

Illustrative material was also obtained from the following sources:

Anheuser-Busch Incorporated, Boatmen's Bank, Chamber of Commerce, Dorrill Photographic Company, Guggenheim Productions, Jefferson National Expansion Memorial, Miss Dena Lange's picture collection, *Life Magazine,* McDonnell Aircraft Corporation, Missouri State Capitol, Monsanto Chemical Company, Eric P. Newman Numismatic Education Society, Office of the Mayor of the City of St. Louis, Old Cathedral, *St. Louis Argus,* St. Louis Medical Society, St. Louis Mercantile Library, St. Louis Zoological Garden, Scottish Rite Cathedral Library, Strauss Photographers, Wabash Railroad.

Beebe, Lucius and Clegg, Charles, *The American West,* New York, Dutton, 1955.

Blum, Daniel C., *Great Stars of the American Stage,* New York, Greenberg, 1952.

Handy, William C., *Father of the Blues,* New York, Macmillan, 1951.

Scharf, J. Thomas, *History of Saint Louis City and County,* Philadelphia, Louis H. Everts and Co., 1883.

Without the Parsons Blewett Memorial Fund, which provided scholarships for the writers, the project would not have been possible.

William Clark ⚜ Nicholas DeMenil ⚜ James Eads ⚜ William Greenleaf Eliot ⚜ B.

Eugene Field ⚜ David R. Francis ⚜ Ulysses S. Grant ⚜ W.C. Handy ⚜ William T.

Henry Kiel ⚜   ⚜ Pierre Laclede

Merriwet   rles Lin

Manuel   J.B. C.

James McDonnell   ⚜ Annie M.

A view of the riverfront in 1930. All the buildings within the
white line were razed for the Jefferson National Expansion Memorial.

John Berry Meachum ⚜ Stan Musial ⚜ John O'Fallon ⚜ John Peck ⚜ Josep

John Queeny ⚜ Willam M. Reedy ⚜ Thomas Riddick ⚜ Dred Scott ⚜ Isaiah Sellers

Foreword

This year of 1964 marks two centuries of tempestuous life in our St. Louis since it was named for a revered French king by those bold founders of the tiny fur trading post in 1764, the man Pierre Laclede and the boy Auguste Chouteau. That story and others are the nostalgic heritage of our children today, and it is the responsibility of our schools to transmit that heritage, hopefully with the help of this collection of tales of our past.

Like the other great cities of our land, our metropolis has been clawed by bulldozers, scored by new highway networks, patched by enormous housing complexes. Thousands of new citizens have thronged into the city while other thousands have departed. All of our children need to belong securely to their urban environment, need to tap stakes of personal identity into a community which will soon be theirs. Only if they succeed in doing so — through an awareness of our history — can they help achieve the destiny envisioned by its founder when, two hundred years ago, he said:

"I have found a situation where I am going to form a settlement which might become hereafter one of the finest cities in America."

William T. Sherman ⚜ William Sublette ⚜ George Vierheller ⚜ Carl Wimar ⚜ Willi

William Ashley ⚜ Baptiste ⚜ William Beaumont ⚜ James Beckwourth ⚜ Thome

Susan Blow ⚜   ⚜ Grace Bumbry

August B   bert Car

Charless   Chou

Pierre Chouteau ⚜   ⚜ William Clar

Model of riverfront

Nicholas DeMenil ⚜ James Eads ⚜ William Greenleaf Eliot ⚜ Bernard Farrar ⚜

David R. Francis ⚜ Ulysses S. Grant ⚜ W.C. Handy ⚜ William T. Harris ⚜ He

Apology

We couldn't put in all the great
Or even all the small,
And many names with sterling claims
We haven't used at all.

But here's a rather varied lot,
As anyone can see,
And all and each by deed and speech
Adorned our history.

Some got the medals and the plums,
Some got their fingers burnt,
But every one's a native son,
Except for those who weren't.

So praise and blame judiciously
Their foibles and their worth.
The skies they knew were our skies, too,
The earth they found, our earth.

Rosemary and
Stephen Vincent Benet

From: A BOOK OF AMERICANS by Rosemary and Stephen
   Vincent Benet, Holt, Rinehart and Winston, Inc.
Copyright, 1933, by Rosemary and Stephen Vincent Benet.
Copyright renewed, 1961, by Rosemary Carr Benet.
Reprinted by permission of Brandt and Brandt.

Pierre Laclede ❦ Merriwether Lewis ❦ Charles Lindbergh ❦ Manuel Lisa ❦ J.

James McDonnell ❦ Annie Malone ❦ John Berry Meachum ❦ Stan Musial

John O'Fallon ❦   ❦ John Pec

Joseph Pu   John 2

Reedy ❦   omas

Flag of St. Louis. Blue and white lines rippling through a background of red represents the meeting of the Missouri and the Mississippi rivers at St. Louis. The gold bezant at the symbolic confluence of these rivers bears a blue fleur-de-lis, heraldic symbol of our city's French heritage.

Dred Scott ❦   Isaiah Sellers

Henry Shaw ❦ William T. Sherman ❦ William Sublette ❦ George Vierheller ❦ Car

William Ashley ❦ Baptiste ❦ William Beaumont ❦ James Beckwourth ❦ Thom

Contents

St. Louis
Begins

FOUNDING OF A CITY

One August morning in 1763 a man and a boy led a band of frontiersmen up the Mississippi River from the French town of New Orleans. They had loaded their boats with tools and trading goods and food. They were beginning a long journey to find a place where they could start a new business — fur trading.

The man was Pierre Laclede, a Frenchman who had come to the New World eight years before. The boy was Laclede's trusted helper, Auguste Chouteau — age thirteen.

About three months later they reached Ste. Genevieve, where Laclede wanted to set up his trading post. But this town was too small. It had no place to store his supply of goods.

With winter coming on, the river would soon be filled with ice. Laclede had to move on. Then a message came from the commander of Fort de Chartres. Laclede and his men could spend the winter there and store their goods in the fort's large warehouse.

1

At Fort de Chartres Laclede heard bad news. France, which had been fighting with England, had lost the war. The French would have to give up all their land on the east side of the Mississippi to the English. Laclede and young Chouteau made several trips across the river to find a good place for their fur-trading post. They were determined to build it on French land.

Laclede was unaware that the west side of the river did not belong to France either. It was part of the great piece of land called Louisiana. Some time before, France had secretly turned over all this territory to Spain to keep England from getting it.

One December morning Laclede and Chouteau crossed the river through floating blocks of ice. They tied up the boat and set out on their search. It turned out to be a long hike — through underbrush, up hills, and down into valleys — to the spot where the Missouri River flows into the Mississippi.

The return trip was faster, for Laclede had made up his mind. The place he had chosen had all that a fur-trading post needed.

The two climbed a hill. Standing near a spot where the Old Courthouse is today, Laclede showed the boy why this would be a good place to live. There was a bluff near the water's edge to form a natural dike. Floods would not

be a problem. There were paths, too, one on each side of the bluff, leading down to the river, and on the shore itself was a good landing place. There were timber for houses and prairie for farmland. There was even a small stream where a dam could be built. The falling water would turn the wheels of a flour mill.

Laclede turned to Auguste. "Here," he said, "are all the advantages one could desire to found a settlement which might become considerable hereafter. . . . As soon as navigation opens you will return here and will cause to form a settlement after a plan that I shall give you."

He cut down some trees and blazed others to mark the spot. Then the two travelers, man and boy, returned to Fort de Chartres. Laclede reported to the commander:

"I have found a situation where I am going to form a settlement which might become hereafter one of the finest cities in America."

When the ice in the river at Fort de Chartres began to break, Laclede fitted out a large boat with supplies and put it in Auguste's charge. On the boat were thirty men, including farmers, millers, carpenters, and one blacksmith. With this small band, on February 14, 1764, Auguste Chouteau landed at what is now the foot of Market Street. Years later, a granite marker was placed there.

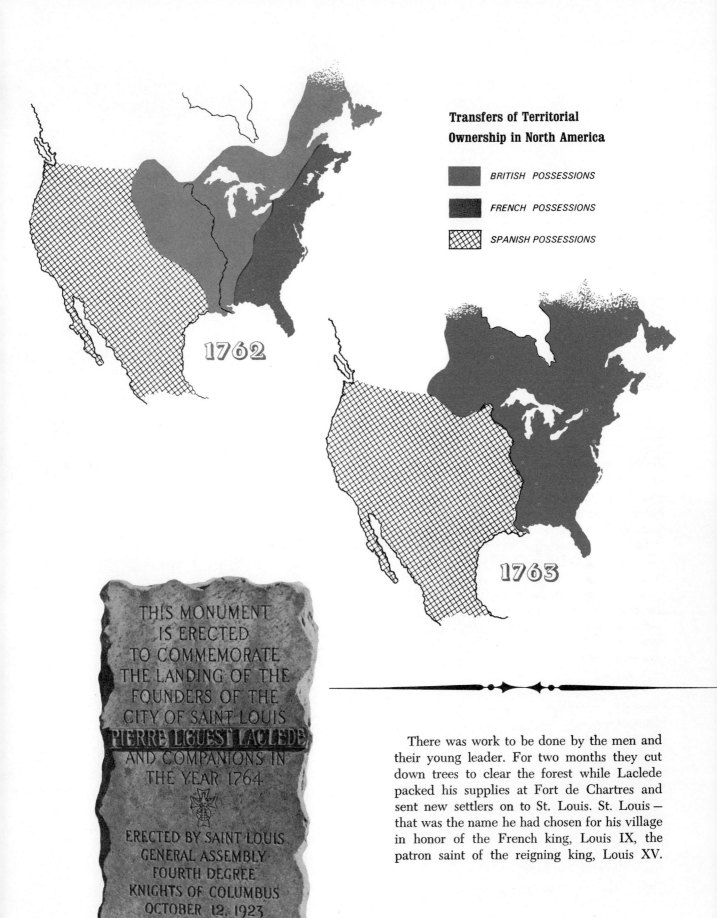

Transfers of Territorial
Ownership in North America

BRITISH POSSESSIONS

FRENCH POSSESSIONS

SPANISH POSSESSIONS

1762

1763

THIS MONUMENT
IS ERECTED
TO COMMEMORATE
THE LANDING OF THE
FOUNDERS OF THE
CITY OF SAINT LOUIS
PIERRE LIGUEST LACLEDE
AND COMPANIONS IN
THE YEAR 1764

ERECTED BY SAINT LOUIS
GENERAL ASSEMBLY
FOURTH DEGREE
KNIGHTS OF COLUMBUS
OCTOBER 12, 1923

There was work to be done by the men and
their young leader. For two months they cut
down trees to clear the forest while Laclede
packed his supplies at Fort de Chartres and
sent new settlers on to St. Louis. St. Louis —
that was the name he had chosen for his village
in honor of the French king, Louis IX, the
patron saint of the reigning king, Louis XV.

3

CHOUTEAU POND

6

MISSISS

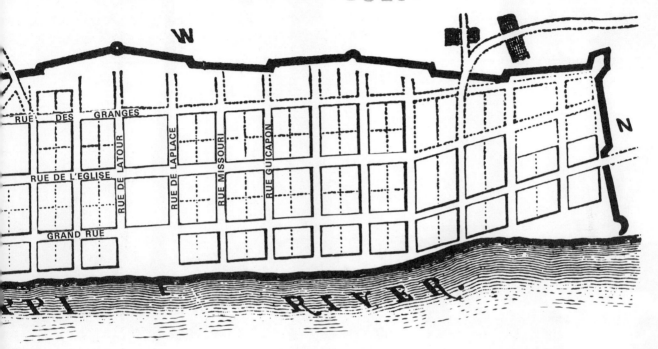

LAND UNDER CULTIVATION

W

N

RUE DES GRANGES

RUE DE L'EGLISE

RUE DE LATOUR

RUE DE LAPLACE

RUE MISSOURI

RUE GUICAPON

GRAND RUE

RIVER

As he had promised, Laclede made a plan for his newly named settlement. Here is a drawing of his plan.

Laclede's little village lay between the streets that are now Lombard and Franklin. Space for a public square was marked off in the center. You will find it on the map at the river's edge, with a square for Laclede's own house behind it. West of Laclede's home was a square for a church. A church was soon built there, and from that time to the present there has always been a church on that ground. The Old Cathedral stands there now, on the only piece of land in St. Louis that has never been sold.

Three long main streets ran in the same direction as the river. The French word for *street* is *rue*. The street nearest the river was named *Grand Rue*, later Main Street. Then came *Rue de l'Eglise*, or Church Street, where the church was to be built, later called Second Street. The Street of the Barns, *Rue des Granges*, became Third Street.

East-west streets were marked off on each side of the center square. *Rue de la Place*, the first one on the north, became our Market Street. The French words for the others were later changed to names of trees, such as Walnut, Chestnut, and Pine.

To the west of the squared-off blocks, a fertile area was set aside for common fields. The land was to be divided into long narrow strips, which the villagers would use for farms and gardens.

Young Chouteau followed the plan carefully. He and his men built the houses first. Even before they were finished, Auguste's mother brought her four other children to the new settlement. Soon other settlers came from across the river.

Auguste Chouteau, Sr.

Madame Chouteau

Pierre Laclede

Gentle Madame Chouteau was like a mother to the new village. In her fine home, on Main and Chestnut streets, she entertained important guests.

This picture shows her in a plain gray everyday dress with a kerchief around her head. You may see the original, done on wood, at the Missouri Historical Society. You can see pictures of Pierre Laclede and Auguste Chouteau there also, as well as a red coat that Auguste wore, a dress of his bride's, and glassware that belonged to Laclede.

About fourteen years after the founding of St. Louis, Pierre Laclede died while traveling up the Mississippi on a return trip from New Orleans. He was buried in an unmarked grave on the river's bank. Auguste Chouteau died at the age of seventy-eight, 65 years after he had helped found the city. His tomb can be seen in Calvary Cemetery.

Living in St. Louis today are many descendants of Auguste, his brother Pierre, and his three sisters. Families named Chouteau, Clark, Walsh, and Bates are only a few of them.

The Oldest Known Picture of St. Louis

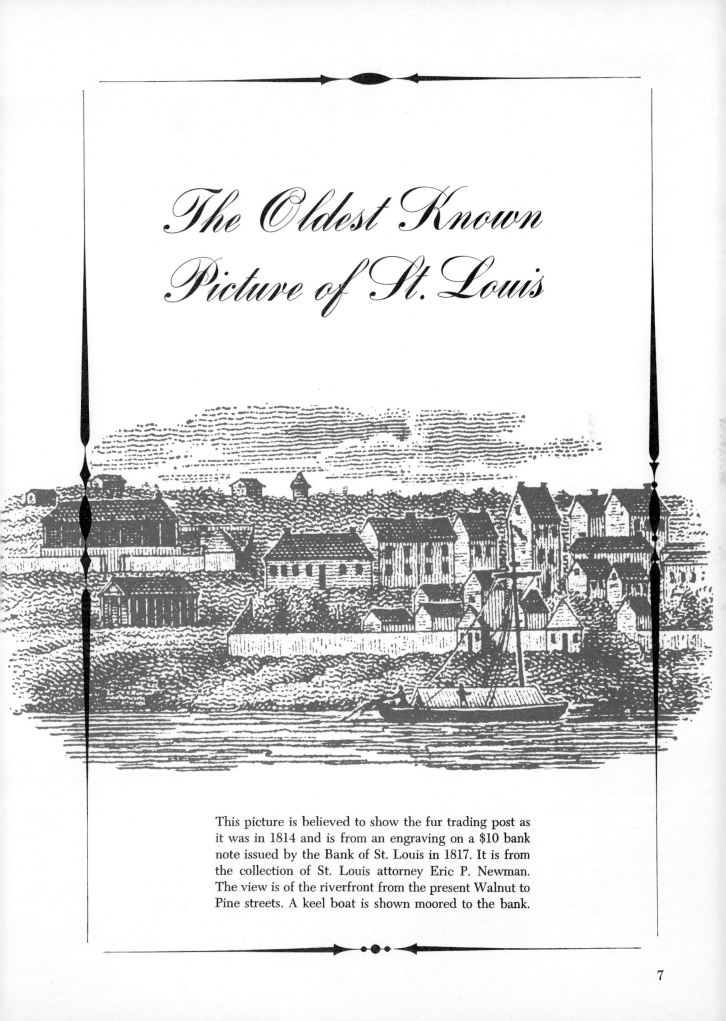

This picture is believed to show the fur trading post as it was in 1814 and is from an engraving on a $10 bank note issued by the Bank of St. Louis in 1817. It is from the collection of St. Louis attorney Eric P. Newman. The view is of the riverfront from the present Walnut to Pine streets. A keel boat is shown moored to the bank.

A present-day map of St. Louis shows great changes in Laclede's village. The Jefferson National Expansion Memorial, on the Riverfront, stretches from Poplar Street to Washington Avenue. From the river it reaches to Third Street, which is now a great highway connecting the downtown area with north and south St. Louis.

Many of the east-west streets remain, but they begin at Third Street rather than at the river. Market is one of them. Others are Chestnut, Pine, Olive, Walnut, Elm, and Spruce — all named for trees. Still other street names are those of early St. Louisans, such as Gratiot, Clark, Papin, Lucas, Labadie, and Berthold. Cerre Street was named after Chouteau's wife, who was Marie Thérèse Cerré.

The names of the founders appear frequently as we tour St. Louis today. Chouteau Avenue begins near the river and runs all the way to Forest Park. On Laclede Avenue, east of Grand, you can see the LaClede Park Apartments. A tall office building in Clayton, on Hanley and Forsyth, is called the Pierre Laclede. At 4440 Lindell Boulevard stands an older apartment house, the Pierre Chouteau, named after Auguste's brother and nephew. A statue of Laclede stands between the City Hall and the Municipal Courts Building. Some of you see "Laclede School" on the sign in front of your school building at 5821 Kennerly Avenue, or "Chouteau School," if the address is 1306 South Ewing.

But perhaps the best remembrance is the Riverfront Memorial itself. With boundaries almost the same as those of the original village, it is a lasting reminder of Laclede and Chouteau, the founders of St. Louis.

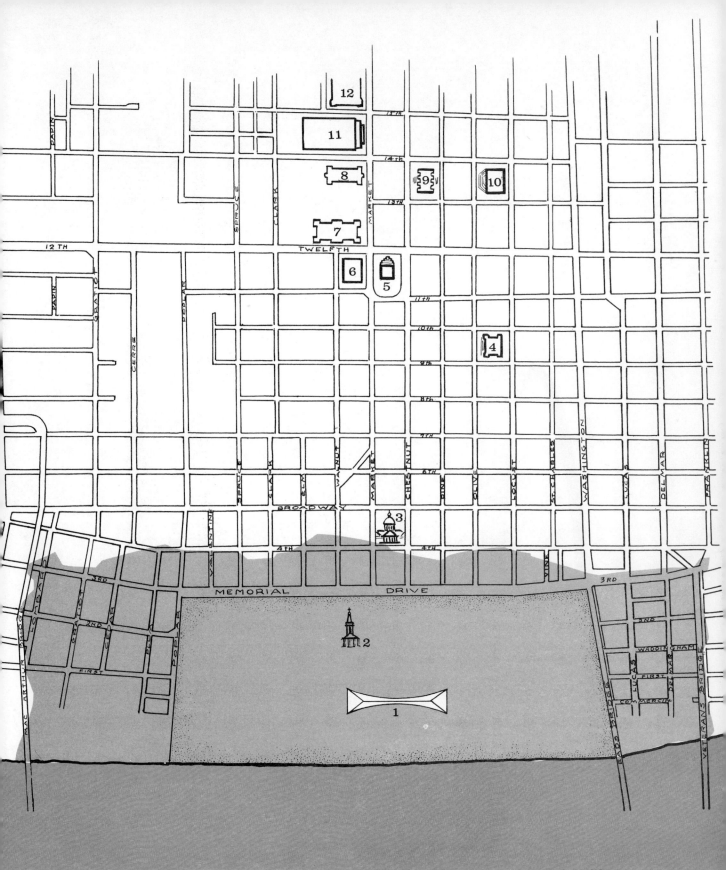

Part of Present-Day St. Louis Showing Boundaries of Laclede's Village

1. Gateway Arch
2. Old Cathedral
3. Old Courthouse
4. Old Post Office
5. Civil Courts
6. Federal Building
7. City Hall
8. Municipal Courts
9. Soldiers' Memorial
10. Public Library
11. Kiel Auditorium
12. New Federal Building

KING LOUIS / SAINT LOUIS

In front of the Art Museum, overlooking Forest Park, stands the statue of Louis IX of France, our city's namesake.

Louis Valois IX was born in 1214 and became king of France twelve years later when his father, Louis VIII, died. Until he was old enough to reign, France was actually ruled by his mother, Queen Blanche of Castille. Queen Blanche was Louis's counselor and tutor. Under her guidance he developed wisdom, character, and a religious zeal which made his reign outstanding.

France was a much smaller country then than now and was surrounded by larger and more powerful neighbors. Within France the nobles fought each other, weakening the country. Many of the young men were on crusades to save the Holy Land from the Mohammedans. The men and money they required weakened the country further.

Through all this trouble, Louis ruled well. He kept his subjects from fighting one another; he kept the peace with the neighboring countries; he was charitable to his poorer countrymen; and he was humble in the eyes of the world. During his reign churches and many public works were built in France. In Paris, he sponsored the National Library and the Sorbonne University.

But in 1270 Louis set out on his second Crusade to reclaim Jerusalem for the Christian Church. Only a few weeks after leaving France, his army was swept with the plague. Louis also was stricken and died muttering the word, "Jerusalem."

In an age when most Kings cared only for the good their countries could do them personally, Louis strove for the good of his country. It was natural that he would be a candidate for sainthood. The people thought it was only right when, twenty-seven years later, he was canonized by the Church.

One of his biographers summarizes his character in these words: "Saint Louis stands in history as the ideal king of the Middle Ages. An accomplished knight, physically strong in spite of his ascetic practices, fearless in battle, heroic in adversity, unyielding when sure of the justice of his cause, energetic and firm, he was indeed 'every inch a king.'"

Baptiste

The most sensational court case in early St. Louis history began in 1785. Madame Chouteau's Negro overseer, Baptiste, discovered two runaway Indian slaves near her property. The Indians had deserted and fled from the village a month earlier, taking other slaves and, in addition, horses, blankets, guns, and ammunition from their former masters. They had set several buildings ablaze as they made their escape. Some remained in the village of "the little hills," now St. Charles, but two came into St. Louis to get some other slaves to go away with them.

Baptiste saw two runaways that evening and ran fast to the home of Joseph Papin, son-in-law of Madame Chouteau, to tell him the news. One of the slaves was Papin's. Papin, who did not have Madame Chouteau's permission to use her slave, told Baptiste to keep the runaways there until he could get assistance and arrest them. Papin took a moment to go to the home of his brother-in-law, Sylvester Labadie, to inform him of the matter. Labadie rushed to the lieutenant-governor to tell him and to ask for more reinforcements. The lieutenant-governor immediately sent two detachments from his company. Papin divided his men and the militia. He took some with him and sent the others around by a passage to the fort, warning them all not to shoot except in self-defense. In the excitement, however, some shots were fired and Baptiste was killed.

Madame Chouteau was angry because Baptiste had not been protected. She immediately sent a letter to Governor Cruzat asking his authority for payment of her loss. She wrote that Baptiste's services were invaluable to her. He had so many good qualities that money could not make up for his loss. She asked that Papin be compelled to pay the sum of $1,000.

The whole village of St. Louis was buzzing about the case because of the three well-known families involved. Not knowing how to decide the case, Governor Cruzat referred it to a superior court in New Orleans. The court ruled that the owners of the runaway slaves must pay for the killing of Baptiste since he was helping in the capture without Madame Chouteau's knowledge. She did not get the $1,000 she asked for, but her two sons-in-law and four men were fined six hundred silver dollars. She received payment from the governor sixteen months later.

Under Three Flags

In 1800 Napoleon, in a secret treaty, forced Spain to give France all of its land west of the Mississippi River. Three years later, at war with England and in need of money, he sold this French Louisiana Territory to the United States. But Spain had never officially given the property to France, and this had to be done before the Americans could take possession.

On March 9, 1804, at St. Louis (the capital of Upper Louisiana) Captain Amos Stoddard, a young American army officer, received the land in the name of France from the Spanish governor, Don Carlos de Hault de Lassus. The flag of Spain was lowered and the tricolor of France was raised in its place. At the request of the French citizens of St. Louis, Stoddard allowed their flag to fly for one last day over the village. On the morning of March 10, it was replaced by the Stars and Stripes as Louisiana was officially added to the United States. Within twenty-four hours St. Louis had been under three flags.

A diorama at the Old Courthouse, reproduced above, shows the first step in the transfer—the lowering of the flag of Spain.

13

Flatboat and two keelboats

Meriwether Lewis

EXPLORING THE UNKNOWN

William Clark

The United States had just made the biggest purchase of land in history. We had bought Louisiana from France for $15,000,000. To explore this great unknown land President Jefferson chose his secretary, Army Captain Meriwether Lewis. Lewis picked his old friend William Clark, a redheaded man of action, for his lieutenant. Both were well-fitted for their job. They had had experience with the Indians and were not afraid of hardship and danger.

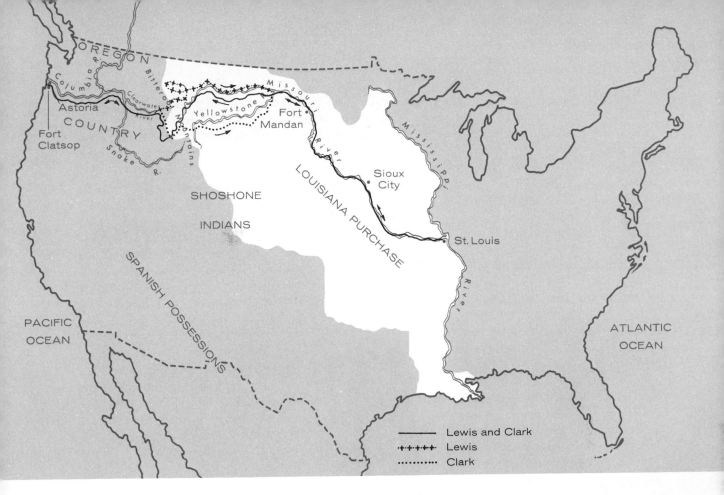

The two young men arrived in St. Louis — the gateway to Louisiana — and quickly moved across the Mississippi to set up a winter camp near what is now Wood River, Illinois. There, opposite the mouth of the Missouri River, the men they had gathered for the journey trained for the life ahead of them. They learned to set up camp and to shoot quickly and well. They made equipment they would need on the trip — kettles, nails, knives, and tools.

During the winter, Lewis and Clark often visited St. Louis to purchase supplies for the expedition. Dr. Antoine Saugrain, a physician and scientist, told them what medicines to buy and gave them homemade matches and thermometers.

At last everything was ready. On May 14, with Captain Clark in command, forty-five men in a long keelboat and two flatboats started up the Missouri River. Captain Lewis finished some business in St. Louis and joined the expedition in St. Charles six days later. The journey lasted two years, four months, and nine days, and the explorers traveled eight thousand miles.

On each of the boats were oars, long poles, a sail, and coils of rope that were fastened to the deck. While some of the men rowed, others pushed the boats forward with the poles. If the current was too swift, part of the crew jumped to the nearby shore and dragged the boats through the water with ropes. When the wind filled the sails, the work was easier.

The travelers went up the Missouri to its source in what is now Montana. Crossing the Bitter Root Mountains, they arrived in Idaho. Then, by way of the Clearwater River, the Snake River, and the Columbia River, they reached the Pacific Ocean.

As the President had wished, Lewis and Clark made careful notes about this new part of the country — its rivers, its mountains, and its plant and animal life. Clark often drew pictures of what he saw.

To gather information about the Indians was an important purpose of the expedition. Luckily, most of the tribes were friendly. Many times the explorers stopped at Indian villages along the Missouri. After giving out presents of colored beads, knives, paints, and blankets, they held councils at which they smoked the pipe of peace with the villagers. During the visits they made long lists of Indian words and their meanings.

15

The travelers spent an entire winter near the homes of one friendly tribe—the Mandans. Here they added three more to their number — a Canadian trader named Charbonneau, his wife Sacajawea, and Baptiste, their month-old son.

Sacajawea, the Bird Woman, was a Shoshone Indian from the Rocky Mountains, who had been captured by the Mandans as a child. This brave young woman was a great help on the journey. Once the boat she was on overturned, pitching passengers and important equipment into the river. With her baby on her back, she clung to the boat with one hand. With the other, she grabbed the objects that were floating by. Drenched but calm, she saved almost everything of value!

Since Sacajawea knew the language of many tribes or could make herself understood in the sign language, she helped the explorers make friends with the natives. Often, too, suspicious Indian bands let the expedition pass peacefully just because there was a woman along.

In the Rocky Mountains, where the rivers were not deep enough for travel, the explorers needed horses. Here Sacajawea was particularly helpful. This was the land of her people, the Shoshones, and the chief turned out to be her brother. He was glad to supply the expedition with horses and a guide.

Sacajawea,
the Bird Woman

In spite of Sacajawea's help, there were many hardships on the long journey. High on the list was the weather. Sometimes the nights were so cold that soldiers could do guard duty for only a half hour at a time. One December dawn the thermometers read 45° below zero. Months later, the summer days were almost unbearably hot, but the temperature went down with the setting sun. Some nights the ink froze on the explorers' pens.

Prickly pears, or cactus, also caused trouble; one night Clark pulled seventeen thorns from his feet. Sometimes swarms of mosquitoes, flies, and gnats tormented the travelers. Sickness plagued them for weeks at a time.

Wild animals, especially grizzly bears, were another worry. Clark decided that he did not

like "these gentlemen and would rather fight two Indians than one bear." Even worse, there were no animals at all on one stretch of the journey. The starving expedition ate dogs bought from the Indians and roots dug by Sacajawea.

But there were happier times too. Often in the evening the men sang to tunes played by their fiddlers. Staring Indians watched them grab one partner after another in a strange performance called a square dance. After months of travel, the men were overjoyed when they tasted salt in a river and knew they were nearing the sea. One happy day Clark made a note in his journal that was poor in spelling but rich in meaning: "Ocian in view. Oh the joy!"

The travelers built a log fort near the Pacific Ocean and spent the winter there. Then they began the long trip home. On September 23, 1806, they reached St. Louis, the city that had almost given up hope of ever seeing the explorers again. Wild with excitement, everyone turned out to meet them. Pierre Chouteau welcomed the two leaders to his home.

The next morning Lewis and Clark were up before daybreak, working by candlelight on reports of their journey for President Jefferson. Since there was no post office in St. Louis, they sent their papers to Illinois, where the mail was held up to wait for them.

The days that followed were filled with parties and dinners. Night after night the pair of leaders sat up late telling of their travels. Fur traders, naturally, had hundreds of questions to ask about lands, rivers, and animal life of the West. Next came a trip to Washington to report to President Jefferson. Lewis and Clark took with them an Indian, Big White, whom they had brought from the West to meet the "Great Father" — the President of the United States. Pleased with their work, Jefferson soon made Lewis the Governor of Louisiana Territory and Clark, Indian Agent. Later Clark became Governor of the Missouri Territory.

After their return, Lewis and Clark made St. Louis their home. Clark married a girl from his

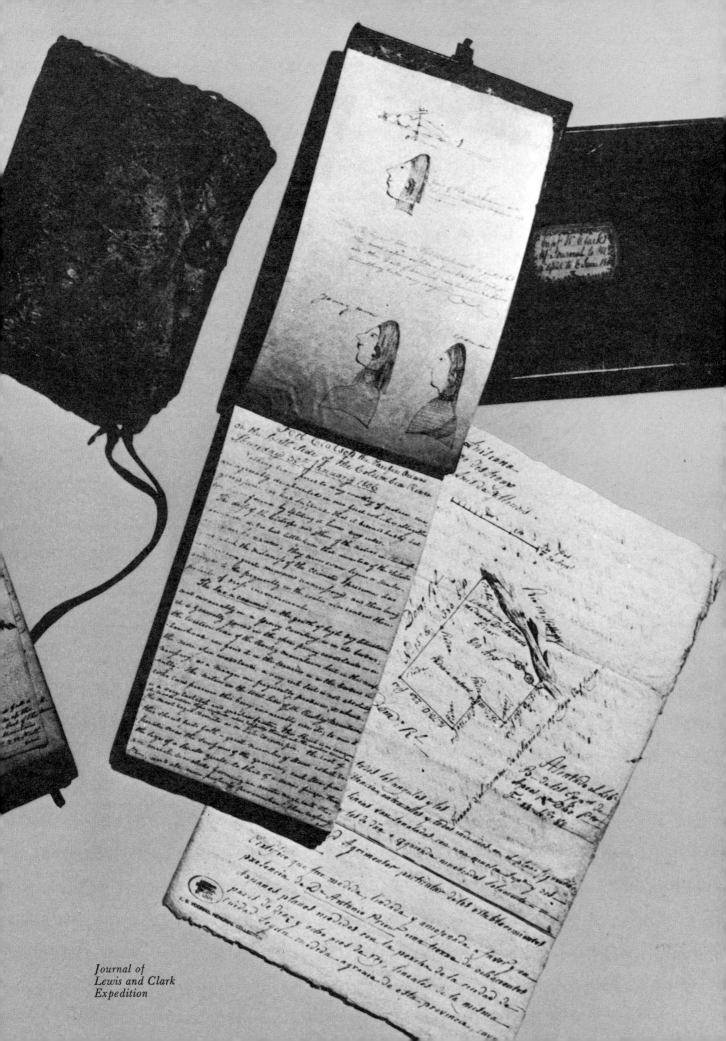

*Journal of
Lewis and Clark
Expedition*

home town in Kentucky and rented a house here on Main and Pine streets.

Lewis and Clark worked for months on the diaries and maps from the trip. When the journal was nearly finished, Lewis decided to take it to the President in Washington. On the way he stopped overnight at a small house in Tennessee. During the night two shots rang out, and the next morning he was found dying. The mystery of his death was never solved.

Clark and his wife were greatly saddened by the loss. Clark could never speak of it, even to his children or his friends. A young lawyer named Nicholas Biddle helped Clark finish the journal, which is now in the Missouri Historical Society Building. You can see photographed pages of it there, with careful drawings by Clark. Other Lewis and Clark objects are on display there too, among them powder horns, a rifle, and a watch that Lewis used on the trip.

All the rest of his long life Clark was the "Redheaded Father" to the Indians. Every spring crowds of them came to St. Louis with their families. Clark met them at the waterfront with presents and took them to the house he had built on Main and Vine. There, in a big room called the Council Chamber, they told him of their troubles. The Redheaded Father listened patiently and politely to their long speeches. Later, with their problems solved, they sang and danced in the St. Louis streets. Through his understanding, Clark saved many lives by keeping the Indians friendly.

When Clark died in 1838, people lined the streets for blocks as his long funeral procession passed by. He was buried on the grounds of Colonel O'Fallon's home on Bellefontaine Road. Later his body was moved to Bellefontaine Cemetery. You can see his monument and statue there.

WILLIAM CLARK
BORN IN VIRGINIA
AUGUST 1, 1770
ENTERED INTO LIFE ETERNAL
SEPTEMBER 1, 1838
SOLDIER, EXPLORER,
STATESMAN AND PATRIOT
HIS LIFE IS WRITTEN
IN THE HISTORY OF HIS COUNTRY.

Today, on a vacation tour, you can follow the trail of Lewis and Clark quickly and comfortably. Near Sioux City, Iowa, there is a monument to Sergeant Floyd, the only explorer to die on the long trip. At Mandan, North Dakota, is a partly restored village of the Mandan Indians. A copy of Fort Clatsop, where the explorers spent a winter, can be seen near Astoria, Oregon.

St. Louis has many reminders of Lewis and Clark too. Clark Avenue (a downtown street south of Market), the Clark School (at 1020 North Union Boulevard), a tablet at Broadway and Olive marking the place where Clark died, the Lewis and Clark Bridges, Lewis Street in southeast St. Louis, and Lewis and Clark Boulevard in northwest St. Louis County — all these recall the brave pair who explored the Louisiana Territory and made St. Louis the Gateway to the West.

Catholic Church in 1776

FAITH
MOVES
WESTWARD

Laclede and his fur traders brought no priest with them, but about two years after the city's founding, Father Sebastian Meurin from Kaskaskia (across the river and downstream) visited the new village of St. Louis. A tent served as his chapel. By 1770 the first log church stood on the land where Laclede had planned for it. Two years later Father Valentine arrived from New Orleans to become the first resident priest.

In 1774 Father Valentine got Spanish Governor Don Pedro Piernas to build a new log church and to donate a bell into which 200 shining Spanish silver dollars had been melted. That bell, which you can see in the Old Cathedral museum, could be heard throughout the little village. Before the new building was finished, Father Valentine mysteriously disap-

peared. Soon afterwards a new priest, Father Bernard de Limpach, blessed the new church. For thirteen years Father Bernard faithfully served his pioneer parishioners. The simple church was used as the place of worship for forty-four years.

During these early years, St. Louis was a part of the diocese, or church territory, of Louisiana and the Floridas, governed by a bishop in New Orleans. In 1815 Father Louis DuBourg (for whom DuBourg High School is named) became the bishop of this territory. Deciding to govern his Louisiana Diocese from St. Louis, he began to round up helpers. Father Felix de Andreis (De Andreis High School) and Father Joseph Rosati (Rosati-Kain High School) were among the new recruits.

19

On January 5, 1818, Bishop DuBourg arrived in St. Louis. He found the old wooden church in ruins and much too small. Within three days he drew plans for a third church. This one was to be a brick cathedral. The cornerstone was laid the same year, but this cathedral was never to be completed.

From the beginning all of the north half of the church block not occupied by the church was used as a cemetery. Although the first burial record found in the Old Cathedral Register is dated 1770, there are civil records showing a number of burials before that date. Before the graveyard was finally closed, almost two thousand people had been buried there. In 1823 the city trustees passed a law against burial of the dead within the city limits. All of the dead were removed from the cathedral graveyard and reburied elsewhere. Many of the graves of these early St. Louisans can be seen in Calvary and Bellefontaine Cemeteries today.

Father Rosati, the first bishop of the newly formed St. Louis Diocese, planned a new and larger cathedral. He and his people agreed that the old partly built cathedral started by Bishop DuBourg, with its unfinished walls and bare rafters, should not be enlarged, but that a new cathedral should be built. The project began with a cornerstone-laying on Monday, August 1, 1831. Three years later the cathedral, on Walnut between Second and Third Streets, was finished, and soon after it was dedicated.

Bishop Rosati presided over this diocese until his death in 1843, when a new bishop, Peter Richard Kenrick, was installed. His was a long and active term of office. He put a three-story addition onto the north wall of the cathedral. Through Bishop Kenrick's help the Christian Brothers opened a school there in 1849. During those years the St. Louis population quickly outgrew the Old Cathedral. More than half of the 30,000 St. Louisans were Catholics, and each year, as more people poured into our city, five hundred more members were added to the parish list. The building of more churches was necessary.

Because of this growth and the establishment of new churches, the importance of the Old Cathedral began to fade. Homes in the Cathedral parish were replaced by office buildings and factories. In 1914 when the New Cathedral at Lindell and Newstead was opened for services, the Old Cathedral lost its bishop and became the Church of St. Louis IX, King of France. For many years it was used mainly to serve the religious needs of downtown workers.

A few years ago Cardinal Ritter authorized a complete remodeling of the old structure. The old rectory and brick addition were torn down, a new rectory was built, and the interior and exterior of the cathedral itself were remodeled. The work was completed in 1963.

As far as possible the interior of the Cathedral has been restored. The heavy old altar has been replaced by a smaller one more like the first one. The windows have been returned to their original design. The original box pews had been replaced in 1893 by other pews; these were simply refinished.

On September 20, 1963, Cardinal Ritter formally announced that Pope John XXIII had decreed, in 1961, that the Old Cathedral would be classified as a basilica, a special honor for a church. (There are only fifteen such churches in the United States.) The Old Cathedral received this honor in recognition of the part it played in the spread of Christianity westward from St. Louis. Cardinal Ritter had decided to keep the decree a secret until after the remodeling. The Church of St. Louis IX, King of France, is now officially the Basilica of St. Louis IX, King of France. A basilica may display two symbols representing the honor. One is a kind of umbrella called a conopoeum. It is of red and yellow silk with coats of arms of Pope John XXIII, Cardinal Ritter, Bishop Rosati, and the basilican seal of the Old Cathedral itself. The carrying pole is twelve feet tall with a gold ball and cross at the top.

Oval window discovered during the restoration of the Old Cathedral

Conopoeum

Tintinnabulum

The other is a tintinnabulum. It is a fancy frame of carved wood containing a small bell. It stands six feet high and is ornamented with gold leaf.

And so the city's oldest church has become a part of America's newest national monument. Millions of people will visit the riverfront every year, and the Old Cathedral will again be a lively and busy church.

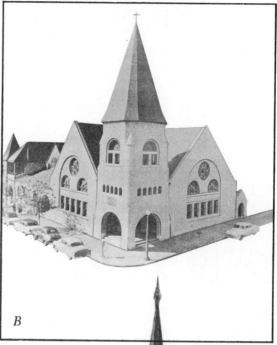

A

B

C

A Diversity of Faiths

A. First synagogue west of the Mississippi and east of the Rockies. Built in 1855.

B. St. Paul's African Methodist Episcopal Church, erected in 1872. First church built by and for Negroes west of the Mississippi.

C. First Presbyterian Church, built in 1824. Occupied by the first Protestant congregation in St. Louis, which still worships in this area.

Some of St. Louis's leading historical figures are buried in Bellefontaine or Calvary cemetery. Many of the graves and tombstones were moved to these cemeteries when the earlier cemeteries had to be destroyed because of the growth of our city. You will recognize most of these names from the stories and may want to visit the graves of these famous people.

CALVARY CEMETERY

Thomas Biddle (? -1831), paymaster at Jefferson Barracks. He was killed in a duel.

Auguste Chouteau (1750-1829), co-founder of St. Louis. In recent years a new table monument has been placed on his grave giving the date of birth as 1740. His birth records in New Orleans and his journal give the date as 1750.

Charles Lucas (1792-1817), lawyer. Son of a wealthy landowner, he was killed in a duel with **Thomas Hart Benton**.

Bryan Mullanphy (1809-1851), Mayor of St. Louis. He is buried on the family lot, which has a beautiful Gothic spire monument.

Dred Scott (about 1799-1858), famous Negro slave, some of whose trials for freedom were held in the Old Courthouse.

William Tecumseh Sherman (1820-1891), General of the Union Army. His grave is marked by a modest, flag-draped monument. His funeral was one of the largest that ever took place in St. Louis.

BELLEFONTAINE CEMETERY

Dr. William Beaumont (1785-1853), an army surgeon. He studied the process of digestion through an open wound in the body of Alexis St. Martin and published a journal of his observations.

Thomas Hart Benton (1782-1858), statesman and patriot. He was a United States Senator from Missouri for thirty years. He favored building a railroad from St. Louis to the Pacific Ocean. On his grave is a small polished red granite monument bearing only his name. A bronze statue of Benton stands in Lafayette Park, and a white marble bust of him is in the Mercantile Library.

Francis P. Blair, Jr. (1821-1875), General in the Union Army. He disapproved of the harsh methods of the Northerners in the reconstruction period after the Civil War. He was a United States Senator. There is a statue of him at the entrance to Forest Park at Kingshighway and Lindell. His grave is marked by a small headstone.

Susan Elizabeth Blow (1843-1916), the founder of the first kindergarten in the United States. At Des Peres School in St. Louis, she began this pioneer kindergarten and trained other kindergarten teachers.

Von der Ahe

Mullanphy

Dred Scott

Eads

Susan Blow

Sherman

Adolphus Busch (1838-1913), a wealthy brewer. His elaborate Gothic mausoleum of pink granite cost about $250,000.

Robert Campbell (1804-1879), important fur trader and wealthy merchant in St. Louis. His home at Fifteenth and Locust streets has been made into a museum. The tall gray granite monument in the center of his lot is a replica of the white marble shaft built there about 1855.

Joseph Charless (1804-1859), founder of the Missouri Gazette, the first newspaper west of the Mississippi.

William Clark (1770-1838), an explorer who traveled to the Pacific Ocean with Meriwether Lewis. A bronze bust of the General looks out over the river. The inscription reads, "Soldier, explorer, statesman, patriot, his life is written in the history of his country . . ."

Wayman Crow (1808-1878), St. Louis merchant, State Senator, and one of the founders of Washington University.

James B. Eads (1820-1887), famous engineer who built the first bridge across the Mississippi at St. Louis. During the Civil War, he built the first ironclad gunboats used in defense of the North. A large marble monument marks his grave.

Bernard G. Farrar (1785-1849), one of the first physicians in St. Louis. A small temple marks his grave.

Davis R. Francis (1850-1927), Mayor of St. Louis, Governor of Missouri, President of the World's Fair, and Ambassador to Russia.

Manuel Lisa (1772-1820), early fur trader of St. Louis and builder of the old Rock House used to store furs.

John O'Fallon (1791-1865), a nephew of William Clark, a wealthy and generous land owner. He founded O'Fallon Polytechnic Institute, which later became a part of Washington University. His monument is a tall granite pedestal on which stands a large figure of the Angel of Hope.

Isaiah Sellers (1802-1864), one of the most famous riverboat captains. The marble bas-relief of Sellers himself was made during his lifetime, and he carried it with him on his journeys.

Chris Von Der Ahe (1851-1913), owner of the first Browns baseball team. His statue above his grave is larger than lifesize; it was erected long before he died. He even had the year of his death placed on the monument while he was still living. It turned out to be the right year.

Charles (Carl) Wimar (1829-1863), St. Louis artist who painted four murals in the Old Courthouse. He was fascinated by Indians, and they were frequently the subject of his painting.

Manuel Lisa

AUGUSTE CHOUTEAU
BORN
SEPTEMBER 26, 1740
DIED
FEBRUARY 24, 1829

FOUNDER OF ST. LOUIS

Chouteau monument

O'Fallon

Busch

Old Courthouse—1844

LAND-
MARK
OF LAW

Old Courthouse today

Most of the land west of the village of St. Louis (that is, west of Fourth Street) was owned by two men, Auguste Chouteau and J. B. C. Lucas. The line between their farms ran westward through the block on which our Old Courthouse stands today. Chouteau owned the land to the south and Lucas the land to the north of this line. In 1816 these owners divided their land into square blocks and gave the block owned jointly to St. Louis for a courthouse "on condition that the ground should be used forever as the site on which the courthouse of the county of St. Louis should be erected." (The city of St. Louis was then part of St. Louis County and was its county seat.) This square was vacant except for a whipping post and stocks for the punishment of wrongdoers. Before this time, court had been held in several rented rooms throughout the city.

The first courthouse building on the square donated by Chouteau and Lucas was started in 1826. By the time it was finished seven years later, it was already too small for this growing community. Plans were made for additions to the existing building that would make it a domed structure with four wings. In 1839 work was started on the rotunda, dome, and west wing. When it was finished, the first building

was torn down, and the present east wing was built in its place. By 1862 a new dome and the north and south wings were completed. It had taken twenty-three years to build our Old Courthouse.

Carl Wimar, the famous St. Louis artist, was hired in 1862 to decorate the newly-completed building with a group of murals. Four of these pictures show historical events: "The Discovery of the Mississippi River by DeSoto in 1541," "The Founding of St. Louis by Laclede in 1764," "The Attack on the Town in 1780," and "A Western Scene with a Buffalo Hunt." Before he could finish the last one, the artist died of tuberculosis at the age of thirty-four. It was finished by his half-brother, August Becker, who had helped him with the others. Below his murals, Wimar had painted oval portraits of George and Mary Washington, Senator Thomas Hart Benton, and Edward Bates.

A few years ago, artists restoring the murals found that those highest in the dome were beyond repair. In these, painted by Pomarede in 1870, four tall figures represented History, Knowledge, Law, and Instruction. Eight other

Dred Scott

emblems and portraits painted ten years later by Ettore Miragoli were also in very poor condition. To repair these paintings, the pieces of painted plaster were carefully removed and fitted together for copying by a museum preservation specialist. The murals were painted anew on canvases that were fixed to new plaster in the original positions.

Many important public events have occurred in the Old Courthouse. Probably the most famous are the trials of Dred Scott. Scott was a slave who came to St. Louis with his master, Peter Blow, in 1830. He was sold to Dr. John Emerson, an army surgeon, at Jefferson Barracks. From there he moved with the doctor to the state of Minnesota, where slavery was barred. There Dred Scot married, and later he and his wife, Harriet, returned to Jefferson Barracks to serve Dr. Emerson. After Dr. Emerson's death, Scott and his wife were left to the doctor's widow. In 1846 the Scotts sued Mrs. Emerson for their freedom. Their lawyers argued that Scott was really a free man because he had lived in free territory.

The first verdict went against the Scotts, and a second trial took place in 1850. In the

Sale of slaves at east front door of the Courthouse

second trial the verdict was for the Scotts, but in 1852 the Missouri Supreme Court reversed the decision. By this time Scott's owner was John Sanford, Mrs. Emerson's brother. Sanford lived in New York. This meant that citizens of two states were involved, so the suit became a federal court case. It finally went to the United States Supreme Court. A final verdict was given in 1857, stating that a slave was not a citizen and therefore had no right to sue in a federal court, and that Scott had given up his right to freedom by returning to territory where he had been a slave. Sanford transferred the ownership of Scott to Taylor Blow, the son of Dred's original owner. Taylor Blow set Scott free in 1857, ten years after the beginning of his fight for freedom.

The sale of slaves was an unpleasant sight at the east front door of the Courthouse, and many St. Louisans disapproved of these auctions. In 1861 the auctioneers were greeted by a crowd of some 2,000 St. Louisans, who set up such a catcalling and yelling that the buyers and sellers could not hear each other. That sale was called off, and it was the last one ever attempted in St. Louis.

In 1876 the City of St. Louis and the county separated. The city took over the Old Courthouse. In 1930, when the new Civil Courts Building at Twelfth and Market was built, the courts in the old building were officially closed. The judge and lawyers marched in a body to the new building, where the courts were reopened.

After the courts were moved, some of the heirs of Chouteau and Lucas sued the City of St. Louis for the title to the Old Courthouse. They claimed the conditions laid down by Chouteau and Lucas that "the ground should be used forever as the site of the courthouse" had been disobeyed. The Supreme Court decided against the claim.

After the United States Government bought the land for the Jefferson National Expansion Memorial, it seemed a good idea to have the Old Courthouse become a part of this memorial. So in 1940 the city gave this landmark to the United States. Since then the building has been occupied by the National Park Service. Exhibits portraying the history of St. Louis can be seen there today. Two of these displays are "The Closing of the Mississippi" and "Transfer of Upper Louisiana."

The Old Courthouse has been an important part of St. Louis history, and it will be a reminder of that history for many years to come as people from all over the world visit our riverfront memorial each year.

Diorama in the Old Courthouse

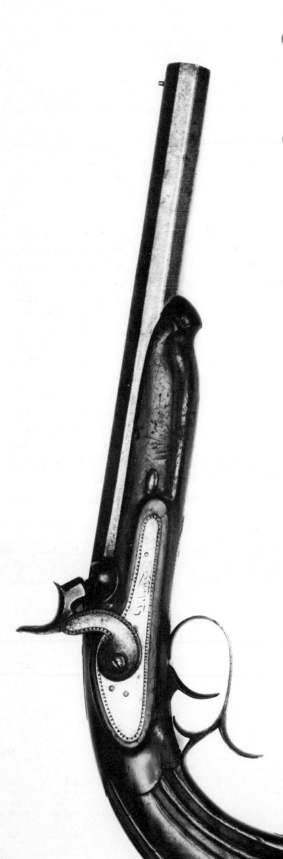

CODE OF
HONOR

Early one spring morning in 1810 two elegantly dressed gentlemen prepared to leave St. Louis in separate boats for a sandy "no man's land" near the middle of the Mississippi River. Dr. Bernard G. Farrar, first English speaking doctor to settle here, sat in the bow of one of the boats. A close friend, James A. Graham, took his place in the other boat. Each carried with him the most deadly weapon of that day, the smooth-bore eleven-inch dueling pistol. In a few minutes they would be standing thirty feet apart, ready to fire at each other.

The man who had caused the duel was not even there. He was Dr. Farrar's brother-in-law, who was accused of cheating at cards during a game with Graham. Even though duels were against the law, Farrar's brother-in-law challenged Graham and asked Farrar to be his second. Because he was a member of the family, Dr. Farrar couldn't refuse. No one knows why the brother-in-law didn't show up to fight his own battle, but Dr. Farrar was forced to fight his friend under the "code of honor."

On shore a group of people, including two police officers, watched the boats disappear into the fog. Minutes later the crack of two pistols was heard. Soon after this the sound of rowing came from the river. The first boat appeared. In the bow Dr. Farrar supported his wounded friend. The doctor's treatment and care were not enough. Graham died a few days later.

The island on which this duel took place became known as Bloody Island. For about fifty years it was a popular scene for such encounters, about a hundred duels being fought there. Because the island, now a part of the Illinois shore, was neither in Illinois nor in

Missouri, the laws of these states did not apply to it.

There were rules for dueling. Each man chose his second. The seconds met and worked out the details. Each duelist made a will and wrote long letters of farewell to friends. Men who refused to duel or failed to appear at the right time were socially disgraced.

One of the most famous duels in American history took place between Thomas Hart Benton and Charles Lucas. Both Benton and Lucas were eager young lawyers. They opposed each other in a legal battle. Lucas claimed that Benton misstated some evidence in his speech to the jury. Benton said this was a direct lie and challenged Lucas to a duel. Lucas refused because he didn't think his actions as a lawyer should affect his private life. But hard feelings existed between the two long after the case was closed. Then one August morning Benton went to a polling place to vote. Lucas was there and asked Benton if he had paid his taxes. This was an insult because a man was not permitted to vote unless his taxes were paid. Benton told the judges that he would answer any questions *they* would ask, but he would not answer to "any puppy who may happen to run across my path." Lucas thought about Benton's words and a week later challenged him to a duel. Benton, as the challenged party, chose the conditions. He picked Bloody Island, the eleven-inch dueling pistol, and a distance of ten paces.

A number of people gathered on the bank as the boats disappeared toward the island. Soon they heard two shots "so close together as almost to seem one." Lucas's shot struck Benton below the knee, but Benton's struck Lucas in the throat. The seconds asked the principals if they were "satisfied." Lucas replied that he was, but Benton shouted loudly and angrily that he was not and demanded another meeting as soon as Lucas recovered.

Six weeks later Lucas had recovered, and again the men faced each other on Bloody Island. Both men fired. Benton was not hurt, but Lucas fell with a fatal wound in his chest. Benton rushed over to the dying man. "Colonel Benton," Lucas said, "you have persecuted me

and murdered me. I cannot forgive you." Benton was quite upset over this until Lucas, realizing that he would soon die, said, "I can forgive you. I do forgive you." Then he died.

In 1820 a duelist named William Bennett was convicted and hanged for murder. The duel in which he fought took place near St. Louis, and his opponent was Alphonse Stewart. Their seconds had agreed to remove the bullets from the pistols. Discovering the plan, Bennett replaced the bullet in his gun. He killed Stewart and was brought to justice because of this unfair advantage, not because of the duel.

Many of the battles were fought over political differences. In 1831 Major Thomas Biddle, paymaster at Jefferson Barracks, fought Spencer Pettis, United States Representative. Pettis, in his fight for reelection, had written a newspaper article criticizing the politics of Nicholas Biddle, Thomas's brother. Major Thomas Biddle was angry. Early one morning he went to the Pettis home, found Pettis still asleep, and began to horsewhip him. Outsiders rushed in and put a stop to the beating. Pettis, of course, called for a duel. But the challenge was delayed until after the election. Biddle had the choice of distance. He was quite nearsighted and chose to stand only five feet away. Their pistols were so close that they could touch. Both men were killed.

Probably the last duel on Bloody Island was in 1860 between General D. M. Frost, commander of Camp Jackson, and Edward B. Sayers, the engineer who planned the camp. Sayers criticized some of Frost's military tactics and a duel followed. On the island Sayer missed Frost, and the general fired into the air.

With the nation involved in a civil war, men found less and less cause to fight "private wars." Dueling began to disappear. Then in 1865 the problem was solved in a clever way. A law was passed stating that anyone who fought a duel, acted as second, accepted or carried a challenge, or went out of the state to fight a duel could not "hold any office in the State." Since most of the duelists were office holders, the law was most effective. Thus ended the practice of dueling in St. Louis.

BEAUMONT *finds a way*

William Beaumont

The winter of 1822 was over at Fort Mackinac, Michigan, a United States army outpost and headquarters of a fur trading company. Thousands of French Canadian boatmen were back from their yearly trip to get furs. One day while some of them were celebrating in the company's store, a shotgun was accidentally discharged. Three feet away, nineteen-year-old Alexis St. Martin, a French-Canadian Indian, slumped to the floor with wounds in his chest and stomach. A shout went up for the army surgeon on the post, Dr. William Beaumont.

When the doctor arrived at the store, he was sure that his patient would be dead in twenty minutes. But he cleaned and bandaged the wounds and sent St. Martin to the post hospital. Under his care, St. Martin slowly got better. But the hole in his stomach did not close. It had to be plugged to keep food from escaping.

For three years Dr. Beaumont took care of St. Martin. Twice a day he dressed the wound. When the hospital could not afford to keep the young man any longer, he moved St. Martin into his own home. His patient grew stronger, but the wound never healed completely.

Dr. Beaumont was glad when he was ordered to Fort Niagara and allowed to take St. Martin with him. He knew that he had the means of studying how a stomach digested its food — a chance that no one had ever had before. But he needed time for experiments and help from other doctors. At Fort Niagara he could get both.

William Beaumont was not a trained scientist. As a boy he had left his home on a Connecticut farm to seek adventure. Finally deciding to become a doctor, he went to Vermont to work for a well-known physician. He swept out the office, washed bottles, put up prescriptions, and went with the doctor on his calls. That had been his only medical school.

At Fort Niagara, Dr. Beaumont asked advice of other doctors and began his experiments. On a silk string he fastened small pieces of highly seasoned beef, raw salt pork, stale bread, sliced cabbage, and other foods. He put the string into St. Martin's stomach. Every hour he pulled it out to see how the digestion was going. In juice taken from St. Martin's stomach he also tested pieces of food. He made careful notes of the time it took each food to digest. Putting a thermometer into the wound, he checked the temperature of the juice and found that it rose very little. The stomach was not a small oven that cooked what was eaten, as some people thought.

Eager for more knowledge, the doctor took St. Martin on a tour through New York State and showed him to other doctors. But St. Martin had grown tired of the experiments. He wanted to live as other people did. One night he tied his belongings into a bundle and went off to his home in Canada.

For several years, from another army post at Green Bay, Wisconsin, Dr. Beaumont tried to find out where St. Martin was. Finally a fur company agent found him and got him to return. Indian wars were going on, and the doctor was busy caring for wounded soldiers. But in his spare time he went on with his experiments. With St. Martin had come his wife and two children. The doctor had to support them all and his own wife and two children on forty-five dollars a month. St. Martin was an unwilling subject, and his wife sided with him against the doctor.

Four years later Dr. Beaumont took a six-month leave to finish the experiments and write a book about them. Sending St. Martin's wife home, he took his patient to Washington, D. C. In 1833, when Dr. Beaumont published his book, it was highly praised. With little equipment, training, or help, the doctor had found out a great many things about digestion. Most important of all, he had learned that the juice of the stomach digests the food that is eaten and that hydrochloric acid is an important part of those juices.

Because many scientists were eager to see

Model of Dr. William Beaumont's cabin

St. Martin, Dr. Beaumont took him on another tour. Then, because the Canadian Indian was so unhappy, the doctor let him go home for a holiday, but he did not return. In answer to Dr. Beaumont's many letters, St. Martin sent word that he "could do better at home."

With this book published, Beaumont went back on active army duty. He was sent to the St. Louis Arsenal as surgeon and medical officer in charge of buying supplies. On July 23, 1833, he arrived by steamboat with his wife and children.

Since the doctor was allowed to carry on private practice, the Beaumonts lived for a time at 123½ North First Street, now a part of the Riverfront Memorial. Three years later they found a more comfortable home on the second floor of General William Clark's Council Hall. Clark, the aging Superintendent of Indian Affairs, had grown too old to carry out his more active duties and had this part of his home made into living quarters and offices.

In the roomy remodeled Council Hall, the Beaumonts entertained many important guests, among them Lieutenant Robert E. Lee, the future Civil War general. Lee had been sent to St. Louis as an engineer to direct the removal of sandbars from the Mississippi River. With his wife and children he spent a month with the Beaumonts, waiting for the Lee home to be ready. After General Clark died, the Beaumonts went on living in the Council Hall. Later they moved to a boarding house on the north corner of Fourth and Walnut streets.

Already famous because of his book, Dr. Beaumont became a successful physician in St. Louis. He was elected president of the Medical Society and made head of surgery at the Medical School of St. Louis University.

After resigning from the Army in 1839, Dr. Beaumont bought a country home with grounds that reached to the present Beaumont Street, but several years later he had to move back into town. A plague of cholera had struck the city; working night and day, he had no time for the long trip from "Beaumont Place." It was hard to find living quarters; only a month before, the Great Fire of 1849 had destroyed many houses. Finally Dr. Beaumont found a vacant house for his family in the block south of the Courthouse.

With the cholera plague over, Dr. Beaumont's life became more peaceful. But one day, four years later, returning from a visit to a patient, he slipped on some icy steps — an accident from which he never fully recovered. On April 25, 1853, William Beaumont died.

You can see his grave and monument if you visit Bellefontaine Cemetery. In the museum of the St. Louis Medical Society there is a display in his honor. Life-size figures show Dr. Beaumont performing one of his experiments on Alexis St. Martin while the patient's Indian wife and one of his children stand at the foot of the bed. St. Louis has never forgotten Dr. William Beaumont. A street, a high school, and a medical building are named after him.

Beaumont Place

WILLIAM BEAUMONT M.D.
BORN
in Lebanon Conn.
NOV. 21. 1785;
DIED
IN ST. LOUIS,
April 25. 1853.

Robert Campbell

FURS and FORTUNES

Robert Campbell was sick. He had had lung trouble when he lived in northern Ireland. Now, in St. Louis, he had it again. Luckily, there were good doctors here, even in 1824, and Campbell went to one of the best. Dr. Bernard G. Farrar had no wonder drugs to work with, no hospital where he could send his twenty-year-old patient. His prescription was simple—he told young Campbell to go west.

This advice really meant to live outdoors; for the West was plains, forests, mountains, and rivers. The prescription worked, and Campbell began to recover. But he did not return to St. Louis.

Campbell had grown to enjoy the vigorous outdoor life, and he joined the fur trading expedition of another St. Louisan, General William Ashley. Ashley was a man with nerves of iron and the skill of a good explorer. Working with him were such men as trailbreaker Jim Bridger and the daring William Sublette. Campbell turned out to be as brave as the best of them.

Fort Laramie, Wyoming — originally built by Campbell and Sublette

Ashley retired a few years after Campbell joined the expedition and returned to St. Louis a wealthy man. He built a home on an Indian mound near the present Ashley Street in north St. Louis. He became an important person in our city and was elected to Congress.

Campbell and Sublette were soon warm friends. When Ashley retired, they became partners, working for the Rocky Mountain Fur Company. Though they made St. Louis their headquarters, they did not sit behind desks and carry on their business from a distance. The West was still their real home. Each year they rounded up tough, sturdy men as helpers and got together huge loads of supplies. With a long line of pack mules carrying the goods, they traveled to meeting places scattered through the West. The route they took had been discovered by Ashley. Later it became the famous Oregon Trail.

At the stops they made, the two partners were met by trappers and hunters who also worked for the Rocky Mountain Fur Company. Campbell and Sublette exchanged the furs these men had collected during the winter for clothing, new traps, gunpowder, and many other needed things. Then they began the long trip back.

Life wasn't easy in that land of sudden storms, buffalo stampedes, and bitterly cold winters. Indian trouble made it harder. Most of the tribes they met were friendly, but some — especially the Blackfeet — were their sworn enemies.

Once when Campbell, Sublette, and their men met a group of savages, they knew that this battle might easily be their last. They made their wills aloud to each other. Then they rolled up their shirtsleeves, grabbed their pistols, and with Sublette in the lead, attacked the enemy.

Southern Hotel

Sublette was shot through the arm during the fight, but, propped up behind a tree, he went on giving orders. The Indians were defeated, and the wills proved to be unnecessary.

Campbell and Sublette were a bold pair in all their deeds and plans. Like mice teasing a lion, they dared to compete with the large and powerful American Fur Company. After a while, the American Fur Company was willing to split the fur-trading country into two parts, so that each company could stay out of the other's way.

Not long afterward, the two partners retired from the fur trade and came back to St. Louis to live. They had made some money, but they had done more than that. Like many other fur traders, they had helped open the West. They had also helped build up the fur trade that, more than anything else, would make St. Louis a great and prosperous city.

Their fur-trading days over, Campbell and Sublette began a different sort of life. For a while they owned a store together. Like all good business men, they knew the importance of attracting customers. They set up a tepee at the store with an Indian family living in it. People flocked to see the unusual sight.

Sublette, remembering his days in the West, bought a piece of land on a hill south of Forest Park, far outside the city limits. There he lived in a stone house filled with reminders of his earlier life. On the grounds he kept a zoo of wild animals that had been captured by Indians and trappers. Like Ashley, Sublette was interested in politics. He wanted to go to Con-

gress from St. Louis. He also wished to be put in charge of Indian affairs, but he died in 1845 while on his way to Washington to see about being appointed. We remember him today because of the street and park that were named for him.

Campbell, in the meantime, went on making money until he was one of the richest men in St. Louis. He became the president of two banks as well as the owner of many houses and lots. His most important piece of property was the original Southern Hotel, which took up almost the whole block from Fourth to Fifth Street and from Walnut to Elm.

He was interested in the affairs of his country too. When the United States went to war with Mexico, he worked tirelessly at getting volunteers and outfitting troops. Because of his life in the West, Campbell was able to serve his country in another way. Though some of the Indians had been his enemies, most of the tribes had always respected him. That was why the government asked him, at two different times, to take part in great councils with the Indians. Today we might call him a trouble-shooter. Through his understanding, many of our Indian problems were solved.

Lucas Place—1854

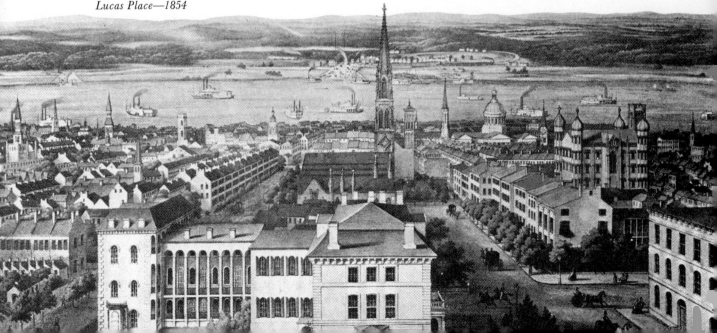

But Robert Campbell's life had another side to it too. In 1837 he met Virginia Kyle, a North Carolina girl. When her relatives heard she was thinking of marrying a St. Louisan, they were horrified. To them St. Louis was the Wild West. It took four years, but Robert finally persuaded Virginia to marry him.

When Virginia came here as a bride, she liked St. Louis immediately. Thirteen years later, in 1854, she must have liked it even better, for the Campbells moved from their home on Fifth and Elm streets to a fashionable new address — Number 20 Lucas Place. Later Robert bought the lot next door to the east, where he built a summer house and a carriage house.

*　*　*　*　*　*

Number 20 Lucas Place is now 1508 Locust Street, and the Campbell home is a museum. There you can see how St. Louisans lived in the 1850's. Inside and out, the tall, prim house looks much as it did when it was a center of St. Louis social life. The living room, with its rosewood furniture and its square piano made in Philadelphia, is especially elegant. At either end of the room a mirror reaches from floor to ceiling, and mirrors top the two marble mantels above the twin fireplaces. Many famous people who were guests of the Campbells saw themselves in those mirrors. Among them were Civil War General William Sherman, bridge builder James Eads, and most important of all, President and Mrs. Ulysses S. Grant.

For the President's visit, Mrs. Campbell made a special trip to Philadelphia to buy beautiful glassware and dishes. Thirty-six people could sit at the big dining room table, and no doubt there were that many when the President came to town. An interested crowd gathered outside the house, and President Grant stepped down the paved walk to the iron fence to speak to them.

Campbell House

Kitchen in Campbell House

Parlor in Campbell House

Rosewood piano in Campbell House

Upstairs, in a glassed-in room, you can see figures dressed in the clothes that were then fashionable. One of them wears the gown that Mrs. Campbell wore in honor of the President. In the bedrooms are large, four-poster beds and great chests, called wardrobes, used to store the family's clothes.

Going down the back stairway, you reach the kitchen with its copper-lined sink, its cupboards, and its wooden chairs. Mrs. Campbell's cookbook is in a glass case on one of the walls. Her recipes tell how to make such things as cupcake gingerbread, stewed crab, and cough syrup. A row of small bells hangs near the ceiling. Guests could ring these bells from their bedrooms when they wanted something from the kitchen. Usually hot water was needed, and servants took it to them in the metal pitcher that stands on a shelf above the sink.

In the yard outside the kitchen is the old pump that provided the water for the household. There, too, in a small garage-like house, is a carriage made by a leading carriage maker of St. Louis and used by Mrs. Campbell.

The Campbell home was greatly loved by the three sons who grew up there. Of all the thirteen children born to Robert and Virginia, they were the only ones who lived past early childhood. When their mother died in 1882, three years after the death of their father, the sons continued to live in the old house. They threw nothing away, and they took great care of every article their parents had used. James died in 1890 at the age of thirty. The two other brothers, Hugh and Hazlett, lived on for many years. Shutting off most of the rooms, they lived in a small part of their home.

When Hazlett died, public-spirited St. Louisans, aided by Stix, Baer and Fuller and Yale University, bought the house, which was about to be sold. Restoring it was an easy task because the brothers had taken such good care of its lovely contents. The old-fashioned home, a strange sight in a crowded business area, tells St. Louisans of today the story of their past.

BECKWOURTH

James P. Beckwourth was a rugged frontiersman, familiar with the wilds of the West. The St. Louis blacksmith joined General William Ashley's Rocky Mountain Fur Company in the fall of 1823. He was a mountaineer for forty years as well as a scout, trapper, trader, and rancher, but was best known as peacemaker with the Indians. Beckwourth spoke Indian dialects, French, and Spanish. He was beloved by the Crow Indians who made him the Chief of their nation. He lived for many years with them until his death. The Crows gave him the full burial of a Chief, wrapping his body in a buffalo skin and hoisting it on a platform into the branches of a tree. His memoirs were published by Harper and Brothers in 1856.

General Lafayette

They Visited St. Louis

Lafayette was coming to the United States! That was important news to Dr. William Carr Lane, mayor of St. Louis in 1824. (Carr Lane School is named after him.) He and the city's aldermen decided that the French general who had helped free our country from England must visit our city, which had been founded by the French. When Lafayette arrived in this country several months later, their invitation was waiting. The general accepted — St. Louis was about to have its first famous guest.

The city leaders had a problem though. There was no money in the city treasury for entertaining distinguished visitors. Mayor Carr Lane came up with a good idea. Why not ask the governor of Missouri to take part in the welcome? After all, this would be an important occasion — and naturally the state should help pay the cost.

The capital of Missouri was then St. Charles. Since the legislature was not in session, however, Governor Frederick Bates was staying at his farm five miles north of St. Charles. The mayor got on his horse and rode out to see him. But Governor Bates refused to have anything to do with the affair. He said that the state had no money for any such purpose.

Mayor Carr Lane returned to St. Louis disappointed but still determined. Talking to some of the aldermen, he found them willing to take money from the treasury and pay it back from their own pockets if the people objected. Leading St. Louisans joined in the preparations. Major Pierre Chouteau (brother of founder Auguste) offered to entertain Lafayette in his elegantly furnished home on Main Street between Vine and Washington. Major Thomas Biddle (for whose family Biddle Street was named) said he would lend his carriage and two beautiful white horses. Two more white horses were promised by Judge James Peck. A reception and ball were planned. St. Louis was ready and waiting.

In the late afternoon of April 28, 1825, a messenger galloped into town. The steamboat on which Lafayette was traveling had tied up at Carondelet for the night and would arrive in St. Louis the next morning. The town crier went through the street calling, "Lafayette is coming! Lafayette is coming!"

Early the next day the people of St. Louis began to gather on the riverfront. Probably no one in the wildly excited crowd was more eager to see Lafayette than an old tavern keeper named Alexander Bellissime, whom everyone called "Old Eleckzan." Over forty years before, he had come with Lafayette from France to fight in the American Revolution. Wounded in the battle of Yorktown and left for dead, he had managed to crawl from the bloody battlefield. Later he had limped his way westward to St. Louis and had made his home among its many Frenchmen. Now, dressed in his carefully brushed old uniform and cocked hat, he waited for his former general.

Shortly after nine o'clock the *Natchez* steamed up to the landing place at the foot of Market Street. Cheers from the crowd and a speech from Mayor Carr Lane greeted Lafayette when he stepped ashore. After

Town home of Pierre Chouteau, Sr.

replying, he was helped into Major Biddle's carriage. Seated with him were Mayor Carr Lane, Auguste Chouteau, and Stephen Hempstead. The two pairs of white horses had never worked together before, and at first they refused to move, but after a while they calmed down and the carriage moved forward. Cheering, shouting, singing, the townspeople followed. A company of troopers on horseback which had been lined up in front of Auguste Chouteau's house at Second and Market streets joined the parade as it started up Main Street. Along the way to the Pierre Chouteau home, an enthusiastic little French boy named Joseph LaBarge dashed out of the crowd. Running to the carriage, he jumped on the rear axle. The crowd gasped at his boldness, but Lafa-

yette was not offended. Gently stroking the child's head, he asked his name. "LaBarge," said the boy. "Ah," said the general; "then we are both Frenchmen and our names are the same — except for their endings."

When the parade reached the Chouteau mansion, the troopers got down from their horses and marched to the porch of the house. Raising their swords, they formed an arch for Lafayette to pass through. The general was introduced to each one.

Then came the moment Old Eleckzan was waiting for. He went up to the general and asked Lafayette if he knew him. But forty years had made too many changes. The general slowly shook his head. Old Eleckzan then told the general about something that had happened on the ship coming from France. Lafayette remembered the incident. Throwing his arms around the old soldier, he hugged him, and they both wept for joy. The watching people wept with them.

St. Louis Riverfront—1843

After a reception at the Chouteau home, Lafayette was taken on a tour of the city. George Washington Lafayette, the general's son and traveling companion, went along. In the vacant square where the Old Courthouse now stands, the St. Louis militia was drilling. The great general who had commanded many grand armies in Europe got out of his carriage and was saluted by some thirty men, many of whom were carrying broomsticks and umbrellas instead of guns.

Next the visitors were taken to the museum where General William Clark kept the Indian curios that he had collected on the famous Lewis and Clark expedition, among them a necklace made of bear claws. Much later, when Lafayette had returned to France, General Clark sent him a gift—a live grizzly bear. The French general's letter of thanks is in the Missouri Historical Society. The grizzly bear was much admired, the letter says, since he was the first animal of the kind that had ever been seen in Europe. Lafayette at first thought of making a pet of the bear, as he was then very gentle. But deciding that this might be unwise, he gave the young grizzly to a European museum, where he developed "a large, vile, and ferocious temper." Clark received a gift from Lafayette too — a camp chest, containing many articles needed for overnight travel.

In the late afternoon the Lafayettes were driven to the Freemason's Lodge on Elm Street between Second and Third streets, where they were made honorary members. Back at the Chouteau home, they ate an excellent dinner at a table loaded with wild fowl and European wines. Then came the grand ball at Bennett's Mansion House Hotel, which stood on the

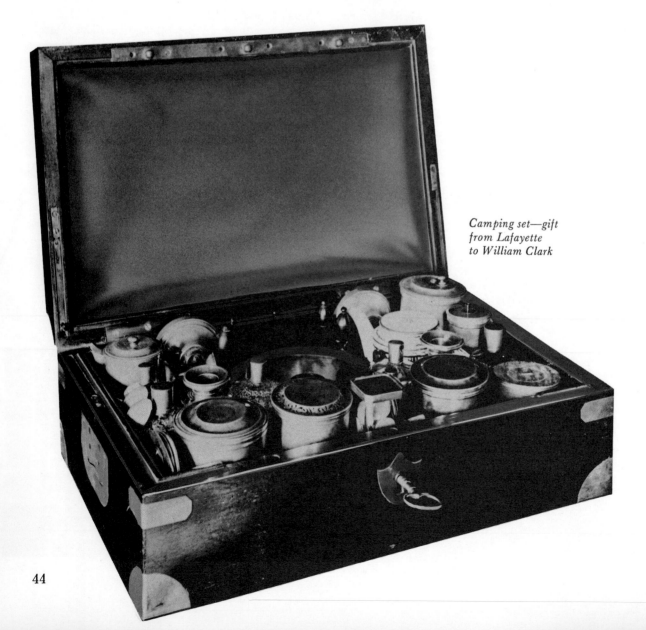

Camping set—gift from Lafayette to William Clark

corner of Vine and Third streets. Many a young lady danced with Lafayette that night; years later, many a grandmother boasted about that dance. After the ball, Lafayette was taken to the *Natchez,* where he slept. Early the next morning the steamboat took the sleeping general down the river. In St. Louis, Mayor Carr Lane added up the expenses. Lafayette's entertainment had cost our city the staggering sum of $37.

Few visitors to St. Louis have made a more lasting impression than Lafayette. Lafayette School, 815 Ann Avenue, is named after him. The first park in our city was named Lafayette in his honor; you can see it today, a city block bounded by Park, Missouri, Mississippi, and Lafayette avenues. Many associations and companies also have the general's name.

Bennett's Mansion House Hotel

Entrance to Lafayette Park

Danl Webster

St. Louis entertained other well-known guests as the years went by. When Daniel Webster, the famous senator and orator, came to the city, every effort was made to impress him. The riverfront was gaily decorated. Piled high on every side were bales of cotton and stacks of material for merchants and the outfitting of expeditions to the West. Fifty steamboats were tied up at the wharves. A cannon was fired when Webster's boat was seen coming, and a brass band greeted him when he arrived. The best carriage in town, drawn by prancing horses, took him to the National Hotel at the southwest corner of Third and Market streets. There he spoke to an admiring crowd gathered in the street. The next day, at a barbecue in Lucas Grove (now Eighth and Chestnut streets), he made a longer speech, which was also well received. When he left on the following morning, St. Louisans were his fast friends.

The Webster School was named for him, as well as Webster Groves in St. Louis County.

Not long after Webster left, a royal guest—King Otho of Greece—visited Pierre Chouteau. Otho was a blond giant six feet four inches in height. Every morning, without fail, he turned up at Chouteau's banking house and silently lounged there for an hour or so. The rest of the day he loafed about the city, playing cards, shooting pigeons, and riding with anyone who was willing to ride with him. At the many dinner parties given in his honor, St. Louisans were shocked by his table manners. They felt that a king could be expected to keep his trailing moustaches out of his soup. When the king's stay began to seem endless, someone managed to have him invited to the town of Ste. Genevieve down the river. Our city named no streets or schools for Otho.

St. Louis gladly welcomed an English visitor in the 1840's — the famous novelist Charles Dickens. But Dickens did not like us and said so later in his writings. He had a long list of criticisms: our weather was too hot; our swampy lands were breeding grounds for disease; our Mississippi River was a dirty ditch. The food at his hotel—the Planter's House (at Fourth and Market)—was good, he wrote, but the prices were much too high and the hotel itself looked like a hospital. St. Louis, to Dickens, was just a western frontier town with pigs and cattle running loose in the street.

Chas Dickens

John James Audubon, the naturalist and artist, spent several days in St. Louis in 1843 and left with mixed feelings. In a letter to a friend, written later, he praised the variety of the foods in St. Louis markets and their low cost. But he could not understand why the Glasgow Hotel, where he stayed, charged such a high price — $9 a week. In contrast, chickens were three for 25 cents, turkeys the same, potatoes 10 cents a bushel, beef 3 to 4 cents a pound.

St. Louis liked another of its royal visitors much better than it liked King Otho. He was the Prince of Wales—later to become King Edward VII of England—but he was traveling under the name of Lord Renfrow. This pleasant lad of nineteen enjoyed the reception and dance given in his honor. He liked the horse race he attended even better. It was held in what was then open country but is now Fairgrounds Park (Grand and Natural Bridge).

There he spent over three hours in the ring, watching trotting races in which the best horses of the United States were entered. A crowd of 100,000 people, including all of St. Louis high society, had come to watch the horses and the prince. A cold meal was served after the races. English reporters who had come with him were amazed by the huge dishes piled with slices of beef, mutton, and buffalo tongue. A dish made from "a sort of cabbage cut into thin slices, raw, and mixed with vinegar" was new to them. It was cole slaw.

John J. Audubon

Grandstand at race track in Fairgrounds Park—1892

They were amazed too, by the sight of St. Louisans eating cold meat with nature's forks—their fingers. Our table manners must have seemed as poor to them as King Otho's had seemed to us. But the Prince enjoyed both the supper and the dance that was held later in the evening. St. Louis enjoyed having the Prince too. Long before the night ended, everyone had stopped pretending that he was a lord. When his steamboat pulled out the next morning, it was followed by friendly calls from those who saw him off: "So long, Prince. Come back some time."

When St. Louisans heard that Henry Clay—the famous Senator and statesman from Kentucky — was coming for a visit, they began excited preparations for his welcome. But Clay sent word that he wanted no receptions or speeches—he was simply coming on business, to sell some of the property he owned here. He had bought it earlier as an investment. Lexington and Ashland avenues in north central St. Louis are named after Kentucky cities because they were a part

of that property, and a street in the same neighborhood is called Clay. The Senator's many St. Louis friends refused to be discouraged, however. They had a cannon set up, and when Clay arrived its mighty booming drew many townspeople from their stores and homes. Before his steamboat could be anchored, an admiring crowd climbed aboard and almost turned the vessel over. Later, when the auction of Clay's property was held at the courthouse, a crowd gathered again. But the buyers were few, and they did not allow their admiration to affect their business judgment. The bids were so few and so low that the Senator had to stop the sale. In spite of this unhappy event, crowds jammed the Planter's House when a ball was given there in the Senator's honor, and Clay said that he carried away only happy memories.

Many other well-known names were on the guest list of early St. Louis. Singer Jenny Lind, President Ulysses S. Grant, actress Sarah Bernhardt, Grand Duke Alexis of Russia — these are but a few who visited this hospitable city.

Time To Learn

READING, 'RITING, AND 'RITHMETIC

In 1764, when St. Louis was a little village, many of the inhabitants were backwoodsmen with little education. They had to know something about hunting, trapping, and farming—but they did not need schools to learn these skills. Some early St. Louisans could not write their own names and signed documents with an X. The leaders, men like Laclede and Chouteau, were well-educated, and had even brought with them enough books for a library. At fourteen, Chouteau had already learned enough to direct the building of the trading post according to Laclede's plans.

Still, the early St. Louisans wanted education, and soon schools began to appear. They were very small schools, almost always run by one man or woman. The very first school was started by Monsieur Jean Trudeau in 1774 in a little one-room house located near the river. It was a private school for boys, and Trudeau taught them in French. Although Trudeau was a good teacher and taught for fifty years, he died a very poor man. Low pay for teachers was common in the early days, not just in St. Louis, but everywhere. Old records show that farmhands were sometimes paid more than teachers.

Class for foreign-born St. Louisans—1903

51

In the next few years other small private schools sprang up not far from Trudeau's. In these the teaching was also in French. The first girls' school was held in a log building on Main Street. It was begun in 1790 by Madame Maria Rigauche. The girls who studied under her had a special reason to be proud of their teacher. In 1780 Madame Rigauche had helped save St. Louis in an Indian attack by encouraging the soldiers, loading muskets, and helping bring in the wounded while the battle was still going on.

Madame Rigauche loved to teach the young girls of St. Louis. Her husband had died, and she needed money badly. She was promised a salary of only fifteen dollars a month, but actually never received that much. Later she received a tract of land as payment.

It was not until 1804 that the first English-language school was opened. Its teacher was a Mr. Rochford. This was also a private school.

There were several forms of private education. Some of the early schools were academies and convent schools. They offered both elementary and secondary school subjects. Sometimes groups of families got together and paid the salary of a teacher for their children, paying so much per child. Other families hired governesses, who lived in the family home while teaching the children. There were also parochial schools, organized by churches and directed by the pastors. Some of the schools taught the ordinary subjects—reading, writing, grammar, and arithmetic. Others taught dancing, sewing, cooking, fencing, and athletics.

All the private schools had one thing in common. They were for people who could afford to pay. Before long, outstanding St. Louisans saw the need for educating all children, even those who could not pay. They knew that in a democracy citizens had to read, write, and figure if they were to govern themselves intelligently. In addition, many working class parents wanted free schools so that their children could improve themselves.

But St. Louis was still in many ways a frontier town, with many problems besides education. It took a very foresighted pioneer to undergo additional hardships for the sake of starting schools. St. Louis had such a man in Thomas Fiveash Riddick. In 1806 much of the land around St. Louis was unclaimed. That is, no individual person owned it, nor was it used as "commons"—fields shared by the villagers for farming. Riddick had the idea that the unclaimed land should be used for the support of schools. If this land could be set aside for education, any money that came in from its rent or sale would help pay for schools.

Early schoolhouse

Thomas Riddick

Riddick was so excited about his idea that he decided to go to Washington himself and explain his plan to the Missouri delegate in Congress. He gathered all the information that he could about the need for schools and about the available land and set off on horseback. Because it was winter the trip was rough and dangerous. Yet Riddick went gladly—and at his own expense.

When he arrived in Washington, Riddick explained his plan to Edward Hempstead, the Missouri delegate. Hempstead promised to introduce a bill that would put the plan into effect. But there were delays—Congress had many other problems to solve. Eleven years after Riddick's ride, in 1817, St. Louis was made a special district, and Congress put aside some land in the district for schools. When Missouri became a state in 1820, Congress again set aside land for schools. But very little money was ever raised from its sale or rental.

Riddick did not get much money for the schools, but his efforts encouraged others to see the importance of education. Without his work, and that of Hempstead, our public schools would have had a much later start. (The Riddick and Hempstead Schools are named after these two men.)

Although no public schools were started for some time, a few people opened private schools that poorer people could afford. Some public funds were used to pay the teachers for the children too poor to pay. These schools had to be run as cheaply as possible. The cheapest school was one which needed only one or two teachers for perhaps several hundred children. This type was known as the Lancastrian school after Joseph Lancaster, who had started such a school in England. The first Lancastrian school in St. Louis opened in 1815.

Another name for this school was the monitorial school. The school might consist of one or two very large rooms. The children sat at rows of benches. There were usually separate classes, or even separate schools, for boys and girls. Before the first class began, the teacher called several monitors up to his desk and taught them the lesson. Each monitor then went to the bench of pupils of which he was in charge and taught them what he had just learned.

With so many children and only one teacher, discipline had to be very strict. The teacher sometimes needed monitors not only to help him teach but to help keep order as well. The teaching was not very good, since it was done by children who barely knew the lessons themselves. But the monitorial schools were cheap, and they existed for many years in St. Louis.

Riddick's famous ride

St. Louis had its first school board in 1833. A school board consists of citizens elected to act for all the people in building schools, hiring teachers, and supervising teaching. The school board had so little money that it could not open a school until 1838.

The first school had two head teachers (called principals), a man for the boys and a woman for the girls. They taught about 350 pupils in two rooms. Soon after the school was opened, the board appointed a superintendent to oversee the work for it. The first superintendent received no salary; his only reward was the thanks of the board.

The first public schools in St. Louis were copied from the private Lancastrian schools. There were two rooms: one downstairs for boys; one upstairs for girls, who made less noise. The teacher's desk was mounted on a platform at the front of the room. Desks for monitors were placed on the platform at either side of the teacher's desk. The public schools were a little better than the old private Lancastrian schools. The large rooms became study halls; to each was attached one or two small classrooms. The principal teacher kept order in the large room and taught one or two classes. The other pupils went to the smaller rooms to recite to assistant teachers or monitors.

In many ways, school life was much different from what it is today. There were no blackboards or paper and very few books. Lessons were sometimes written in sand tables with a pointer. Or they might be written on a long board with the end of a stick charred in the fireplace; when the class was finished with the lesson, the material was "erased" by being shaved off with a plane.

Each teacher was required to keep his room neat and clean. In the beginning he could charge the children for this service. An early school board rule limited the charge to six cents a month per child. Later the children had to do the sweeping themselves. Each child took his turn, and no one was allowed to pay someone else to do the work for him.

Eventually janitors were hired to do the cleaning, but they had other work to do as well. One of their extra duties was to control the children during recess. The janitors also filled ink wells — small bottles of ink, one at each pupil's desk — and kept the pitcher at the teacher's desk filled with water. An 1898 rule prohibited janitors from keeping at school such animals as goats, chickens, and dogs. The only animal allowed was the cat, obviously because of that animal's efficiency as a mouse-catcher.

The school year of the "good old days"

Board of Education, City of St. Louis—1876

might not seem so good today. At first there were only four weeks of vacation—two weeks in winter and two in summer. In 1849 this was lengthened to six weeks in summer—but it was still nothing like our ten- or twelve-week summer vacation. School days were longer, too. In spring and summer, school began at 8:00 A.M. and stopped at 5:00 P.M.; in fall and winter the day ran from 9:00 A.M. until 4:00 P.M.

For a long time boys and girls had to buy their own textbooks, pencils, and paper. It wasn't until 1889 that free books were supplied on a large scale, and then they were given out only through the fourth grade. Sometimes discipline was pretty harsh too, although hitting pupils on the head was against the rules.

Still, both teachers and pupils worked hard to make the schools better. In the 1840's some teachers began teaching night classes without pay. Soon a regular evening school was started. For a number of years German was taught in St. Louis schools, a result of the large number of people in the city who had come from Germany. In 1881 there were more than 20,000 public school pupils studying German. In later years, the school buildings were used on Saturdays for private instruction in German.

Another sign of progress was the establishment of the public high school. During the

Art lesson at L'Ouverture School in the early 1900's

1840's the Board of Education saw that high schools were necessary to make sure that the city would have enough good business men, merchants, lawyers, doctors, and teachers. In 1853 St. Louis opened the first public high school class west of the Mississippi. It was located in Public School No. 3, then called the Benton School. Near the central part of town, the school could be reached by boys and girls riding the horse-drawn omnibuses, which brought them from all sections of the city. Until 1904 there were just two high schools: one for white children and one for Negro children.

The leadership of good school superintendents helped improve the schools. A good example was Ira Divoll, who was superintendent from 1859 to 1867. Divoll worked hard to improve teaching. At that time teachers in St. Louis had an average of fifty-four pupils each. Divoll did his best to lower the number of children in each classroom. He also saw the need for more library books in the schools, and in 1865 he was able to start the first public

Schoolhouse No. 3—Benton School—where the first public high school west of the Mississippi River and probably the first coeducational public high school class in America was opened in February, 1853.

*First delivery wagon
for the Educational Museum
which later became the
Division of Audio-Visual
Education—the first
Audio-Visual Department
in the United States*

school library with 2,000 books. Divoll urged teachers not to spank children severely to get them to behave. Some schools had reported from 100 to 200 whippings per week!

One of Divoll's most important contributions was what he did for the education of Negroes. From the city's earliest days there had been Negroes in St. Louis. They were taught by their owners or in private schools and church schools. When a law was passed in 1847 forbidding the teaching of reading and writing to Negroes, many of the people of St. Louis were indignant. Much of the teaching at home was continued, and some of the schools were conducted under cover. After the law was repealed in 1865, Divoll asked the Board of Education to provide schools for children of African descent. In 1867 three schools for Negroes were opened.

By the turn of the century, St. Louis had one of the best school systems in the world. In 1900 the city won one of five grand prizes at the Paris Exposition for work displayed by elementary and high school pupils. Steady improvement has continued. In 1931 Hadley Technical High School was opened for pupils who wanted to learn various technical trades. Three years later a similar school, Booker T. Washington Technical High School, was started for Negro students. Now, of course, O'Fallon offers such courses to all young people who want to take them. At the elementary level, the St. Louis public school system has become nationally famous for its reading clinics, its Division of Audio-Visual Education, its radio station, and many excellent programs that help more than 110,000 St. Louis boys and girls each year.

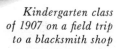

Kindergarten class
of 1907 on a field trip
to a blacksmith shop

Radio Station KSLH,
St. Louis Board of
Education, broadcasting
science program
"Let's Find Out"
to St. Louis classrooms

MAKE A WAY FOR FREEDOM

A dark brown-skinned man placed a bag of coins on the table. The money was for the purchase of a slave. The slave's owner looked at John Berry Meachum with a questioning eye and said, "You want to buy Tom Harrison?" Meachum answered quietly, "Yes, I am going to buy Tom; and after he learns what he needs to know, I will set him free."

Meachum knew that Tom's owner thought it strange that he, an ex-slave, should be buying another slave. It was not strange to John Berry Meachum. He had been born a slave in Virginia. In those days many slaves were apprenticed to skilled craftsmen. He had learned to be a carpenter and cooper or barrel maker. He was thrifty and every time he earned an extra bit of money he saved some of it for a special purpose — to buy his freedom and that of his father.

John Berry Meachum, a free man, moved to Kentucky, where he met and married Myra, a slave woman. In a few years Meachum moved to St. Louis, and his wife's master took her and the children to another part of Missouri.

John Berry Meachum

Meachum arrived here in 1815 with three dollars in his pocket. There was plenty of work for someone who was skilled, and soon he had enough money to buy the freedom of his wife and children and to bring them to St. Louis.

About this time, the Reverend Mr. John M. Peck, a white Baptist missionary, arrived here. The Reverend Mr. Peck had heard about Meachum's unusual plan of buying slaves. The slaves worked in Meachum's cooperage plant, and when they had learned to work well and had saved their money, he set them free.

The Reverend Mr. Peck set up a Sunday School for Negroes. The school taught some reading and writing, but most of the instruction was in sewing, the use of tools, and especially religion. Meachum was a good leader; the Reverend Mr. Peck gave him training in the ministry and ordained him in 1825. Meachum also enlarged his cooperage plant, started a building firm, and eventually built a steamboat which was used to sell supplies to other steamers along the levee.

With the argument over whether slavery would be extended into new territories and the fear of more slave uprisings, a terrible thing happened. The Missouri legislature passed a law in 1847 which definitely prohibited any Negro from learning to read or write. Negroes were not even allowed to hold meetings. Public whipping was the punishment for those who were caught breaking the law and not able to pay the fine. Peck and Meachum went ahead anyway with the worship services and the lessons in reading, writing, and arithmetic. The few books were hidden if the lookout saw a suspicious looking white person coming along.

One day, however, the constable burst into the room where the people were meeting. He ordered them to disband or pay a fine every time they met. He also threatened to take the Reverend Mr. Peck to jail. Meachum and Peck closed the school.

John Meachum did not give up. He set up a day school for the children in the basement of the First Baptist Church which he had pastored since 1827. With an Englishman as the teacher, the church school went on until the authorities heard about it. They came, closed the school, arrested the teacher, and accused him of causing trouble by teaching the Negroes reading, writing, and "figuring."

The Reverend Meachum hired some good lawyers who were able to free the teacher. If he could not get the school one way he would try another. He built another steamboat to use as a school building. This floating school was anchored in the middle of the river. The students went from the bank of the river to the boat in skiffs. No one bothered this school because the river belonged to the federal government. John Berry Meachum's School for Freedom became famous. Teachers from the East came to help him. Hundreds of children learned their Three R's on the Mississippi.

Meachum died in 1854 before slavery and the Missouri ban on learning were abolished by laws, but his name lives on at Meacham Park, subdivision of Kirkwood. For forty years he helped his people — through work, preparation, and education — to win freedom.

William Torrey Harris

Leading the Way

When William Torrey Harris came to St. Louis in 1857, he was only twenty-one years old. His family lived in Vermont, and coming west was a real adventure in those days. At first Harris thought that St. Louis was a terrible place to live. He could not afford satisfactory lodgings, and in his letters to his family he complained about the unpleasant living conditions, including being pestered by mosquitoes and bedbugs. But he was determined to make a go of it.

When he was sixteen years old, he had lost an eye in a firecracker explosion, but he never let the handicap interfere with studying or getting ahead. He taught himself shorthand and he made his own telescope. As a young teacher he used his free time to learn geometry and trigonometry. He also studied German so that he could read German books. In one of his own books he wrote that he took studying very seriously. Each day, he said, he tried to see how many hours of hard work he could get done.

In St. Louis, Harris planned to teach shorthand to private students. This kind of teaching paid very little; therefore, on his father's advice, he took the examination to teach in the St. Louis schools. Teaching was not just a way to earn a living for Harris; he was truly interested in children.

Harris had done so well on the teachers examination that Superintendent Divoll wrote him a very complimentary letter of recommendation and assigned him to start teaching at the Franklin School. This was a model or "normal" school where new teachers could learn by seeing the very best teachers at work. The normal school teachers set the mark or "norm" for beginners.

In his classroom, Harris found almost one hundred and eighty pupils, for the Franklin was a Lancastrian school. They ranged in age from ten to fifteen years, and they were not divided into grades as we know them today. This might have resulted in a mob scene if the school had not been so well organized. As there were four other teachers in this school, Harris did not have to handle all of the children himself.

Harris had never liked the Lancastrian system. The rooms were much too large, the boys had to memorize too much, and the discipline was too strict. Divoll agreed with him, and together they made Franklin a graded school. Divoll and Harris also started teaching boys and girls together in the same classrooms.

Harris was so successful at the Franklin School that the next year Divoll promoted him to principal of Clay School. In those days the principal was also a teacher. Under Harris's teaching the children really liked to study history and science. Harris delighted the children by making a telescope for them, much like the one he had made for himself when he was just a little older than they were. He was in excellent physical condition and did gymnastics right along with the pupils, which impressed them.

Discipline was a problem, however. Harris did not believe in scolding or whipping, so he tried some unusual methods. On his first day at Clay someone warned him about two large, unruly fifteen-year-olds. He sent for the boys and asked them if they would mind going to his home a short distance away to get his dumbbells. If they would do this, he could take his exercise at school. The dumbbells were just heavy enough that the boys returned huffing, sweating, and exhausted. Harris took the bells from them, and before their startled eyes began swinging the bells around with the greatest of ease. The boys caused no more trouble. Later, Clay School became the first in St. Louis to have a gymnasium — and the principal was the star performer.

After a few years as principal of Clay, Harris became assistant superintendent. In this job he visited all of the schools, carefully supervising the work of the teachers and principals. During this time, Divoll and Harris did much of the work which led to the founding of the St. Louis

Clay School

Public School Library in Polytechnic Building.
This was the beginning of the St. Louis Public Library.

Public Library. When Divoll's health failed in 1867, Harris became superintendent of the St. Louis Public Schools.

The schools had problems in those days too. There were not enough school buildings. Children in the primary grades could attend school for only half-day sessions. Teachers taught one group of fifty to sixty children in the morning, and another group in the afternoon. Most children left school after the third or fourth grade. For several years there was a shortage of money, and teachers had to take a cut in pay.

Harris worked hard and solved many of the problems. He told the principals to work with the teachers in improving instruction. Only the superintendent and his assistants had had such duties before. He made the tests to enter teaching harder and added more difficult courses at the normal school.

Harris worried that children left school so young. Many of them quit school after the third grade to go to work. He decided that they should start school a year earlier.

But such young children do not do well in regular classrooms. The schools needed a class designed for young children. About this time a young St. Louis woman, Miss Susan Blow, was studying a new kind of school that had sprung up in Germany. It was called a kindergarten, or children's garden. Miss Blow convinced Harris that the kindergarten would solve the problem of giving children an earlier start. In 1875 he permitted her to organize a kindergarten in St. Louis, and soon every one saw how well it worked. Many more kindergartens began in the years that followed. By starting the kindergarten, Harris helped education all over the United States. It was one of the greatest steps ever taken in American education.

Harris became known all over the world as a great teacher and writer. He left St. Louis in 1889, having been appointed United States Commissioner of Education. In 1905 our city honored Harris by changing the name of the Normal School to Harris Teachers College.

Harris was succeeded by Edward H. Long. Under Long, in 1890, a normal school course was added to Sumner High School, to help train Negro teachers. Later this course was separated from the high school, and a normal school for Negroes was established. Eventually it was named for Harriet Beecher Stowe, a New England writer who had worked hard for the abolition of slavery.

In 1955, when the school system was de-segregated, the two colleges were merged under the name Harris Teachers College.

Harris Teachers College (until 1948). This building now houses the Division of Audio-Visual Education and Radio Station KSLH.

THE SUMNER HIGH SCHOOL FACULTY ABOUT 1900

Seated left to right: Araminta Parker, H. L. Usher, Alice Easton, D. J. Roberson, Helen Burrell, A. W. Scott, Naomi Mitchell.

Standing: Oscar M. Waring, P. H. Clark, A. J. Gossin, E. Campbell.

Saint Louis

PUBLIC SCHOOL SUPERINTENDENTS

Superintendent	Served	Superintendent	Served
George K. Budd	1839	William Torrey Harris	1867
Henry Pearson	1841	Edward H. Long	1880
Edward M. Avery	1848	Louis F. Soldan	1895
Spencer Smith	1849	Ben Blewett	1908
John H. Tice	1852	John W. Withers	1917
A. Litton	1852	John J. Maddox	1921
Charles A. Putnam	1853	Henry J. Gerling	1929
John H. Tice	1854	Homer Anderson	1940
Ira Divoll	1859	Philip J. Hickey	1942
		William Kottmeyer	1964

Susan Blow

*Home where Susan Blow grew up.
Mr. Blow built this home
after the Great Fire of 1849.*

The Children's Garden

Little Susie Blow, just six years old, could sense the anxiety of her parents on that day in May, 1849, as the family fled from its house on Elm Street. This was the day of the worst fire in the history of St. Louis, and the Henry Blow home was in the center of the part that burned.

The Blows never returned to the house again. Instead, Susie's father built a new home in Carondelet, then a little village south of the city. Starting over was not as hard for the Blows as it was for other families. Mr. Blow was a successful business man, who could afford the very best. The new house became known for its solid walnut doors, fine paneled library, and carved marble mantels.

When Susie was about five, she attended a French school for a short time. She did not go to school again until she was ten. From then until she was eighteen she was taught by a governess and at various private schools.

Life in the Blow family was exciting. Many important St. Louisans came to their new house. One of them was their neighbor, Roswell Field, the father of the famous poet, Eugene Field. Susie grew up in the years just before the Civil War. She heard her parents say that no men should be slaves to other men. Many years before, her grandparents had owned a slave whose name was Sam. Sam, later known as Dred Scott, was defended in one of his trials for freedom by Roswell Field.

A future President of the United States, Ulysses S. Grant, delivered cordwood to the Blow home. After he became famous as the victorious Union general, Grant jokingly recalled that once Mrs. Blow had scolded him for scraping the bark from her favorite tree with his wagon wheel while making a delivery. He did not resent the scolding, for later, as President, he appointed Mr. Blow ambassador to Brazil.

With their father a diplomat, the Blow children found life even more interesting and exciting. Susan taught herself Portuguese so that she could be her father's secretary in Brazil. Later the family traveled to Europe, where they met many distinguished people, including members of the nobility. Susan's sister married a Russian count. After Mr. Blow died, the Brazilian emperor and empress visited the Blow home.

This was a strange background for a woman who was to dedicate her life to teaching little children. She did not have to work. She had never even attended a public school, but she was willing to work without pay to show Superintendent of Schools William T. Harris that a kindergarten would succeed.

The idea for the kindergarten originated in Germany with a man named Friedrich Froebel. Miss Blow had read his books, and when she was traveling in Germany, she visited kindergartens to see how they were run. She brought back some of the materials that Froebel's followers were using. These included six solid balls painted with basic colors. There were also cylinders, cubes, and other solid objects, which were used to teach ideas about shapes, sizes, numbers, and weights. In addition, Miss Blow learned the kindergarten songs, games, and plays that were used to teach children about family and community life.

When she returned to St. Louis, she talked to Harris about how valuable a kindergarten would be in St. Louis. He agreed to let her organize a kindergarten in the Des Peres School, a building on south Michigan Avenue that is no longer a school. Although Miss Blow was in charge of the kindergarten, she received no pay. There was one paid teacher and two unpaid apprentices. Miss Blow made the kindergarten a place where children could learn and be happy at the same time.

Early kindergartners salute Friedrich Froebel at Divoll School

On the Campus

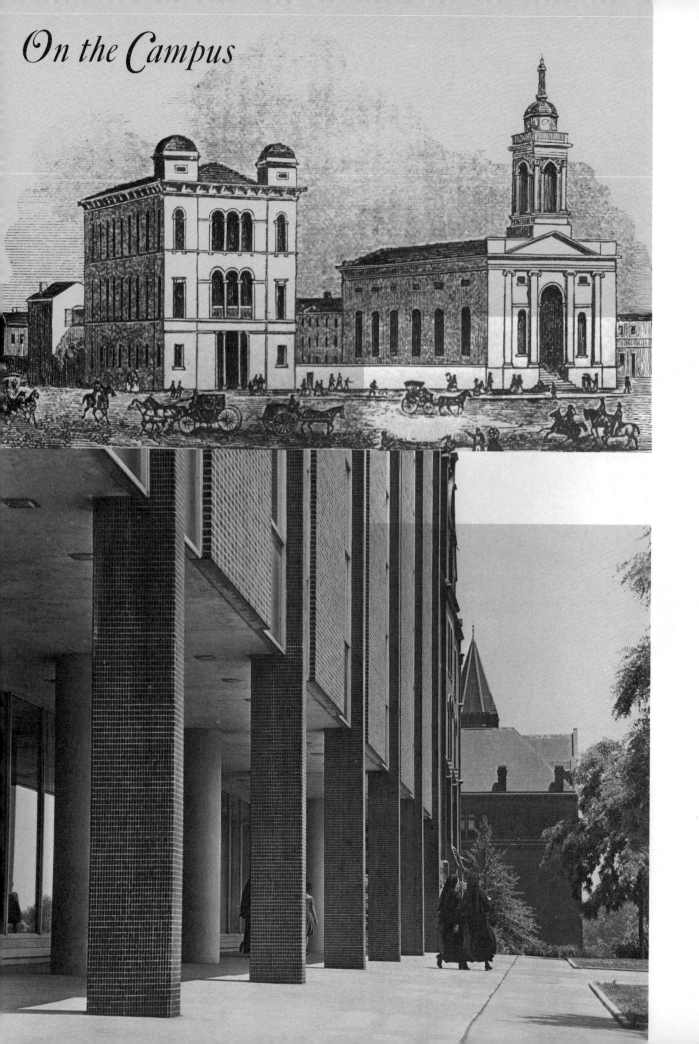

St. Louis University had its beginning as St. Louis Academy, a private school founded in 1818 by Bishop DuBourg, the city's first Catholic bishop. The school's first location was at Third and Market streets, in a house which DuBourg had rented. The good bishop, for whom DuBourg High School in south St. Louis is named, was well qualified to run a school. He had been the principal of a school in Paris before coming to America. When he arrived in St. Louis, he had with him his own collection of eight thousand books, one of the best libraries in America at the time.

ST. LOUIS UNIVERSITY

Two years after starting the school, DuBourg had raised enough money to put up a building for it next to the cathedral on Walnut Street. The name of the school was changed from St. Louis Academy to St. Louis College.

Still, progress was slow. Not many boys attended, and it was hard to get enough good teachers. The first teachers were priests from the local churches, but their pastoral duties prevented them from giving enough time to teaching. For this reason the school had to close in 1826. By that time DuBourg had retired, and Bishop Rosati, who took his place, saw to it that the school was reorganized. When it reopened in 1828, the teaching was done by members of the Jesuit Order, who had come to Florissant in 1823 to set up a school for Indians.

In its early days, the college was really a combined elementary and high school. It was attended by sons of the best-known St. Louis families — Charles Chouteau, for example, who was only eight years old when he enrolled. Other familiar names on the early class lists include Mullanphy, Cabanne, Christy, Papin, and Forsyth.

Under the energetic Jesuits, the school made steady progress. In 1832 it received a charter from the State of Missouri, and its name was changed to St. Louis University. The university granted its first degrees two years later, in 1834.

Today St. Louis University is made up of thirteen schools, colleges, and institutes. The oldest is the College of Arts and Sciences, which dates back to the very beginning, 1818. The Graduate School began when the school became a university in 1832. The School of Medicine and the School of Law are among the oldest special schools. The School of Dentistry was founded in 1903. There are also a School of Nursing and Health Services, a School of Commerce and Finance, and the recently acquired Parks College of Aeronautical Technology.

St. Louis University is many times larger than the tiny school started by DuBourg. Today it has about twelve thousand students. You can see several of its main buildings along Grand Avenue between Lindell and Laclede. A few blocks farther south, across the Grand Avenue viaduct and past Chouteau Avenue, you will come to the Medical School. Opposite, on the west side of the street, is Firmin Desloge Hospital, where the medical students get some of their training.

St. Louis University has been a leader in many ways. Dr. Edward A. Doisy, the head of its biochemistry department, won the Nobel Prize in 1943 for his discoveries concerning Vitamin K. In 1944 it pioneered in the admission of Negro students. A few years ago the university had eleven million pages of books in the Vatican Library at Rome reproduced on microfilm. Students can pick out a reel, put it in a projector, and read a "book" that is a thousand years old and six thousand miles away. Nine thousand of these films, along with more than a half-million books, are available to students at the Pius XII Memorial Library on West Pine.

The president of St. Louis University is Father Paul Reinert, who attended the university himself. Father Reinert is directing the construction of new buildings for the university at Grand and Laclede.

St. Louis sports fans know that the St. Louis Billikens rank among the best basketball teams in the country. The Bills also have fine baseball teams and have been national champions in soccer.

Washington University

Although Washington University was not opened officially until 1857, it had its beginning in 1853. As Eliot Seminary, it was named after the founder, William Greenleaf Eliot, who served as its first president.

From the very beginning, the Reverend Mr. Eliot, a Unitarian minister, hoped that the school would become a university. He talked about this with a friend, Wayman Crow, a wealthy business man and a state senator, who had written its charter. A charter is an official paper from the state that gives an institution its right to operate. Crow also helped by raising money for the school and by making large gifts to it himself.

On February 22, 1853, the trustees first met to discuss the charter; they approved it. They met again on the same day a year later. Since this was Washington's Birthday, they named the school Washington Institute. Four years later, in 1857, the General Assembly amended the charter, making the name Washington University. The founders had several reasons for naming the school after the first President. Washington had served all of the American people, said Eliot, and the new university would be for all people. The university would teach young people to love their country and cherish freedom, just as our first President had done. The university would be democratic. No one could be kept out because of his religion.

Besides Eliot Seminary, there were other schools that later became part of the university.

One was the John O'Fallon Polytechnic Institute, which held evening classes in the old Benton School. This school became the university's first engineering department. Classes were held in the evening because students often worked during the day. Washington University was founded not for sons of rich families, but for those of middle-class business people. Eliot said that a carpenter's shop and a blacksmith's forge were as important to a college student as Greek.

Washington University is well-known for its fine schools of law, engineering, and business. But the medical school is the most famous part of the university. This was not always true. In 1910 a wealthy business man, Robert Brookings, president of the university's governing board, read a report that said most of the nation's medical schools, including Washington University's, were inadequate. He decided to do something about it; he raised $15,000,000. With this money the school put up new buildings, bought equipment, and hired the very best teachers. Since that time the medical school has ranked among the two or three best in the country.

Several medical professors have won worldwide honor. Dr. Evarts Graham was the first surgeon to show that smoking was related to lung cancer. Four other professors have won Nobel Prizes for their discoveries — Dr. Joseph Erlanger, Dr. Herbert Gasser, and a husband and wife, Drs. Carl and Gerty Cori.

The university administration building is now called Brookings Hall, in honor of the man who helped the medical school become great.

This is the familiar building that faces Skinker Boulevard at the west end of Forest Park.

Like St. Louis University, Washington University has grown a lot since its early days. It now has about 13,000 students. Many of them attend evening classes. The school has teams in all major sports—basketball, baseball, football, and soccer. The nickname for the team is "The Bears."

Washington University has had several very famous leaders. In 1946 Dr. Arthur Holly Compton became chancellor. He was one of the scientists who had done the work that led to the atomic bomb. The next chancellor was Ethan A. H. Shepley, a lawyer and business man. Under his leadership the university added the beautiful Olin Library and other buildings. Students from all over the country now live in the new dormitories started in Shepley's administration. Now the chancellor is Thomas H. Eliot, who is a lawyer, teacher, writer, and a former United States Representative. Eliot's grandfather, Charles Eliot, was president of Harvard University many years ago, and Charles Eliot's first cousin was William Greenleaf Eliot, founder of Washington University.

Olin Library, Washington University

The Levee at St. Louis in mid-nineteenth century

STEAMBOAT TO
SPACE CAPSULE

ST. LOUIS – *Queen of the Mississippi*

The golden age of steamboating was in the 1840's and 1850's, and races between boats were frequent. Passengers urged the engineer to raise the pressure until the boilers got so hot that explosions and loss of lives were common. These disasters destroyed scores of boats such as the *Rob Roy, Kate Kearney No. 1,* and the *Glencoe,* but this did not keep the passengers from urging the engineers to go "full steam ahead" when another steamboat seemed likely to overtake them.

The earliest steamboats were not made for racing. Even so, they were an improvement over the flatboats and keel boats which had carried the furs and trading goods up and down the river. They were crude and built much like barges. The cabins were on the lower deck. There were running boards along the side. If the current was too swift, the crew grabbed poles to give the boat more push upstream as the force of steam was not enough. A trip to New Orleans from St. Louis and back, even with the hard work of these rugged men, took from four to six months. They worked to the song of a leader and joined in the chorus to speed away the hours.

The first steamboat to appear in St. Louis was the *Zebulon N. Pike*. It landed at the foot of Market Street on August 2, 1817. The boat was not much over 100 feet long (about three times the length of your classroom). A big paddle wheel turned on either side of the boat, and the wood-burning boiler poured thick black smoke through the single smokestack. Everyone in town was down on the riverfront that day, including a group of Indians. As the boat approached, the fire and smoke from the furnaces scared the Indians and they ran. They thought it was a flaming monster coming up the river.

For a long time there were no boatyards in St. Louis, but near Pittsburgh, Pennsylvania, hundreds of steamboats were turned out in a year. Improvements were made in construction, machinery, size and style of hull and cabin. The early steamboats were small and had only one engine. The later ones frequently were 350 feet long. They were sharp and trim. They had two engines and fancy chimneys on the top. The 1832 steamboat had one deck — the elegant 1860 steamboat often had four or five decks piled up like layers on a birthday cake.

These boats were very luxurious. On the upper decks the staterooms for the passengers had the best furniture and rugs that money could buy. All kinds of people traveled on steamboats. There were gold seekers, Indians and fur traders, immigrants, pioneers, and homeseekers. There were plenty of people to wait on the passengers, and even a band to provide music for dancing. Food was the best. Down below, on the main deck, the deckhands worked hard. On this deck were the boiler furnaces with stacks of wood and piles of coal to keep the fire going. Freight was stored on the main deck and down in the hold below.

With boiler explosions so common, Congress finally required engineers and pilots to take an examination to get a license. Even with trained men running them, the average life of

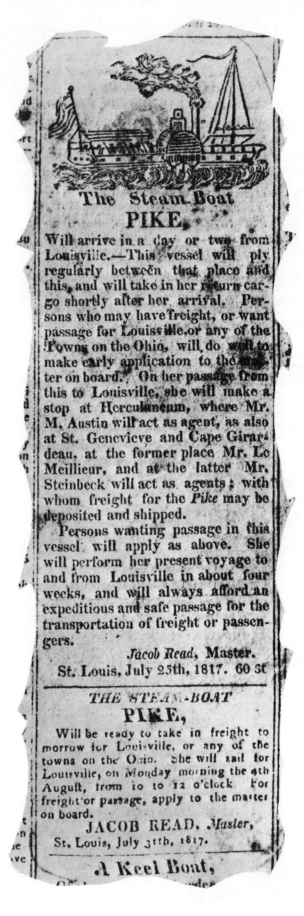

The Steam-Boat
PIKE,

Will arrive in a day or two from Louisville.—This vessel will ply regularly between that place and this, and will take in her return cargo shortly after her arrival. Persons who may have freight, or want passage for Louisville, or any of the Towns on the Ohio, will do well to make early application to the master on board. On her passage from this to Louisville, she will make a stop at Herculaneum, where Mr. M. Austin will act as agent, as also at St. Genevieve and Cape Girardeau, at the former place Mr. Le Meillieur, and at the latter Mr. Steinbeck will act as agents; with whom freight for the *Pike* may be deposited and shipped.

Persons wanting passage in this vessel will apply as above. She will perform her present voyage to and from Louisville in about four weeks, and will always afford an expeditious and safe passage for the transportation of freight or passengers.

Jacob Read, Master.
St. Louis, July 25th, 1817. 60 3t

THE STEAM-BOAT
PIKE,

Will be ready to take in freight tomorrow for Louisville, or any of the towns on the Ohio. She will sail for Louisville, on Monday morning the 4th August, from 10 to 12 o'clock. For freight or passage, apply to the master on board.
JACOB READ, *Master,*
St. Louis, July 31th, 1817.

A Keel Boat,

The Steamer Republic. *Notice the ornate wood carving, chandeliers, and rugs.*

steamboats was only five years. Since a good boat cost from $100,000 to $150,000 and took eight months to build, owners often chanced losing all their money on the tricky Mississippi. There were snags to rip the bottom out of a boat, changes in channel to run the boats aground, and thousands of miles of everchanging river for the pilots to keep track of. Still the number of steamboats increased. By 1846 there were about 1200 boats on the Mississippi.

The pilot steered the boat. When he sent an order down from the pilot house, the men followed through in a hurry. They never knew when a snag or tree stump might be in the boat's path.

One of the most admired pilots was Captain Isaiah Sellers. Captain Sellers had memorized the 1200 miles between New Orleans and St. Louis so well that he knew every house, barn, shed, and dead tree on the way. Any time of

night he could be called out of his stateroom to the pilot house and tell where he was. He knew exactly where state lines touched the banks. For a period of over 40 years, "Sellers is at the wheel" was the best thing a frightened traveler could hear. He never lost a boat of which he was the pilot and never wrecked a boat by collision.

Sellers wrote notes on shipping for the *New Orleans Picayune* which he signed "Mark Twain." If the steamboat began to scrape over the sandbars, the pilot and every crew member stopped to listen for the cry of the leadsman. He threw out his line marked with leather thongs at six foot intervals to test the depth. Everyone waited anxiously to see if the line showed two marks. If it did, the leadsman cried "Mark Twain," and the boat could once again move ahead.

Captain Sellers was the kind of man who

Tombstone Captain Isaiah Sellers carried with him on his Mississippi River trips

Mark Twain—riverboat pilot and author

would have burned to a cinder at the wheel, if it were necessary, to save boat and passengers. He was a proud man too. His pride displayed itself through his tombstone, which he ordered before he died and kept near him. You can see it now in Bellefontaine Cemetery. It shows a pilot at the wheel with the map of the river's course at his feet.

Another famous pilot on the river also adopted "Mark Twain" as his pen name. This Mark Twain's real name was Samuel Clemens. He was known the world over for his humorous stories based on his knowledge of the river. He wrote of his early days as a boy in Hannibal, Missouri, when he swam in the river and sailed rafts on it. He saw the floods and watched the steamers passing by with their gay passengers. He learned more about the river as a riverboat pilot and later as a newspaper man. We remember him best for his books *Tom Sawyer*, *Huckleberry Finn*, and *Life on the Mississippi*.

In 1849 the riverfront and other old parts of St. Louis were swept by a terrible fire. "The Great Fire" started when a little river boat, *White Cloud*, anchored at the foot of Franklin Avenue, caught fire. Attempts to put out the fire were hopeless, and it spread to other boats. Twenty-eight boats were burned. Sparks from the flames, with the winds rising high, spread to buildings beyond the levee and destroyed 418 businesses and homes of the old city. After this terrible disaster St. Louis was built into an even greater city than before.

Steamboats had been on the river for over fifty years when the famous "Trial of Speed" stirred the world.

THE ROBERT E. LEE AND THE NATCHEZ IN A RACE FROM NEW ORLEANS TO SAINT LOUIS read the headlines all over the country. Wagers on this first real sporting classic were heavy. Bets were made in all the states and even in London, Paris, and Vienna.

Competition between the two crews was fierce. To lighten his boat, Captain John W. Cannon had removed all the windows and doors from the *Lee* as well as the walls from the cabins on the hurricane decks. The *Natchez* was an older boat and was more heavily loaded with passengers and freight. Until they reached Cairo, Illinois, the two vessels steamed along only minutes apart. But there the *Natchez* was delayed five hours because of the fog. Captain Cannon of the *Robert E. Lee* knew the river better and decided to go on in

The Great Fire at St. Louis—May 17, 1849. Total amount of property destroyed was estimated at five million dollars.

Race of the Natchez *and the* Robert E. Lee

spite of the fog. The *Lee* arrived in St. Louis from New Orleans in three days, 18 hours, and 14 minutes. The *Natchez* made it three hours and 44 minutes later.

Through the years steamboats were used for many purposes. They brought passengers up and down the Mississippi and Ohio Rivers on luxurious "floating palaces." They took fur pelts, corn, wheat, rye, barley, oats, and tobacco to the East and returned with iron, glass, hollow ware, and dry goods to the foot of Market Street. Flour, coffee, sugar, spice, and cotton came from the South. Steamboats were used for entertainment too. They were called "show-boats." The circus, horse shows, plays, and musicales were very popular on these richly decorated boats that stopped at river towns.

We can see many treasures of the 'Golden Age of Steamboating' in the River Room at the Missouri Historical Society. But when we stand on the levee today, in front of the Saarinen Arch, we have to imagine the days when St. Louis was the "Queen of the Mississippi." The steamboat made us grow and prosper. But time passed and so did the steamboats. The Eads Bridge brought the railroad overland but killed the steamboat passenger traffic by doing in three days what it took the steamboat a week to do.

Old Planter's House in the 1850's

S̶t. Louis hotels became famous throughout the nation in the golden age of steamboating. The Lindell, the Southern, Barnum's, and the Planter's House were all popular. So many people went up and down the river that all of the hotels were overcrowded. Many travelers had to remain on board the riverboats in ports so they could have a place to sleep. The Planter's House at Fourth and Chestnut (across the street from where the Old Courthouse now stands) was built especially to serve the big plantation owners who came from "down south" with their families and servants to spend the winter season.

THE IRON HORSE MOVES IN

St. Louis in 1849 was a brisk, prosperous little river town. Steamboats crowded the levee and money was flowing into the city. St. Louisans were so proud of their steamboats that they were not worried about the rapid development of railroads in the East. Other cities could work hard to get the railroad, but St. Louis was doing very well with its trade up and down the Mississippi River.

Almost overnight St. Louisans were made to see the need for the railroad. GOLD had been discovered in California. Chicago, because of its trade with the West, was growing rapidly. St. Louis had to build railroads to trade with the East and West as well as with the North and South or take second place.

Thomas Hart Benton—Senator from Missouri for thirty years

Statue of Benton in Lafayette Park

United States Senator Thomas Hart Benton introduced a bill in Congress in 1849 which would make St. Louis the eastern end of a railroad to the Pacific Coast. (He was the man for whom Benton Park and Benton Elementary School were named. You may also see his statue, done by Harriet Hosmer, in the middle of Lafayette Park.) Later that year, Mayor James G. Barry of St. Louis called a meeting at the Mansion Hotel, near Third and Vine, to consider building a railroad to the West. Over a thousand representatives from twelve states attended. The meeting did not go well. Senator Stephen A. Douglas of Illinois was the chairman but resigned when he found that because of this office he could not speak in favor of Chicago. Senator Benton was the main speaker at a mass meeting held at the Old Courthouse. He impressed the audience with the words, "Let us build the iron road and build it from sea to sea. Let us ask Congress to build this great road with San Francisco at one end, St. Louis in the middle, and Washington and New York at the other." Then Benton pointed to the West and exclaimed, "There is the East, there is India." India meant new riches. With a railroad to the West, America could trade with Asia as well as Europe. His speech helped the men at the convention decide that the railroad would be a national one. Its branches would be to St. Louis, Memphis, and Chicago.

The people of Missouri were enthusiastic about the Pacific Railroad but had very little money. There was no help from the eastern "big money men" because they had put their confidence and capital in the railroads leading to Chicago. The money for the St. Louis branch had to stretch a long way. Grading, bridges, and tracks were done as cheaply as possible. The construction was poor. This led to poor service, wrecks, and higher costs of maintenance and operation.

One rainy November day in 1855, the St. Louis branch of the Pacific Railroad began its first trip to the capitol at Jefferson City with a special excursion. On the train were important dignitaries, including Mayor Washington King, as well as musicians, soldiers, and St. Louisans from all walks of life. The fourteen-passenger coaches had just reached the bridge over the Gasconade River when the wooden trestle work between the east bank and the first pier went down. One of the passengers described what happened as follows: "I was sitting in the middle car, seventh from the front and rear. The train was going at the rate of 12 or 15 miles an hour. There was a bump, a check to the motion, a cry from someone near, 'We're gone.' Except for the fizzing of

First locomotive west of the Mississippi being unloaded at the St. Louis levee in 1852

the engine, there was a moment of dead silence, save the patter of the rain on the roof of the car, and then cries and groans to tear the heart." Some thirty St. Louisans were plunged to their death and almost an equal number were seriously injured. Fortunately, there were fewer and fewer accidents of this kind as improvements were made.

It is no wonder that people were fearful of the noisy, soot-belching piece of machinery. In the 1850's many people felt that "it just wasn't fitting that a person rush over the country at fifteen miles an hour." But in the years before the Civil War new lines were added and, during the war, the railroad proved how easily it could move great quantities of

Senator Benton delivering his famous railroad speech in the Old Courthouse

John O'Fallon—promoter of Missouri railroads and first president of Missouri Pacific, Baltimore and Ohio, and Wabash Railroads

81

The Union Station was dedicated September 1, 1895. It is another tie with our French ancestry. Theodore Link, the architect, went back to the Middle Ages for his inspiration. He made the building similar to an ancient town in southern France. The railway station, he felt, was a means of entrance and exit like the forts of the Middle Ages. Another unusual feature is the 230-foot campanile on the outside of the building. This bell tower has four illuminated clocks on it, each ten feet in diameter.

As you look inside you will see the Grand Hall, the Terminal Hotel, Fred Harvey restaurants, ticket counters, waiting and lounge rooms, the head house, train sheds, baggage rooms, and a mail building. There are also a building used by express companies, a power house, and an immense concourse.

The Grand Stairway leads to a huge balcony. At the top of the steps on the north wall is a beautiful glass mosaic picture with three female figures representing San Francisco (the West), St. Louis (the Midwest), and New York (the East). These figures symbolize the joining of the three cities by rail. Nearby are the new additions: the beautiful Red Room and the Louis IX Room, which are used for receptions, dinners, parties, and dances.

Across the street from the Union Station is the Aloe Plaza with its magnificent fountain that has become, in recent years, just as famous as the terminal. Entitled "Meeting of the Rivers," it is the work of Carl Milles, world-renowned Swedish sculptor. It is composed of fourteen bronze figures which symbolize the meeting of the Missouri and the Mississippi rivers. The group of statuary, unveiled in 1940, shows the Missouri River represented as a young woman touching her hair. Approaching her is the figure of a young man with a flower in one outstretched hand. He represents the Mississippi. Around the two central figures are three smaller statues and various sea animals. From the mouths of the various sea creatures water spouts high into the air, forming fascinating patterns. Sometimes, if the wind is blowing, you may get a refreshing spray from this fountain.

supplies and troops. During the war, construction of railroads was difficult; track and road equipment were often blown up.

The first railroad station in St. Louis, really a shed belonging to the Pacific Railroad, stood on the west side of Fourteenth Street near Poplar. The trains ran all the way to Kirkwood. When the railroad facilities were extended to Hermann, Missouri, a larger depot was built at Seventh Street near Poplar. After the Civil War the Union Depot at Twelfth and Poplar was built and did a booming business. Into the depot came the Missouri Pacific, the Ohio and Mississippi, the Union Pacific, the Santa Fe, the Kansas Pacific, and the North Missouri Railroad, which we know as the Wabash. By 1889, a number of leading citizens saw the need for a bigger and better station. They got together to form the Terminal Railroad Association, raise money for a new terminal, and devise a rate system for the use of Eads Bridge.

The Association decided to build the station at Eighteenth and Market. Chouteau's Pond, which had been there for many years, had to be drained. In its place the Association built a long row of sheds to cover the many trains that they expected to come to the terminal. The finished station covered so much track that if it were laid in a single line it would have been three and a half miles long.

The Eads Bridge and connecting tunnel brought in more and more trains. The tunnel was intended to carry trains off the bridge and through downtown St. Louis to Union Station without upsetting the flow of traffic. Beneath the old Post Office on Eighth and Olive was a special platform to load and unload mail. You can see this platform today, but it was never used because the smoke and dirt made delivery of mail impossible. You can even feel the vibrations if you are in the old Post Office when a train comes through the tunnel.

Aloe Plaza Fountain

A Bridge to the West

James Eads

Thirteen-year-old Jim Eads and his mother found themselves in St. Louis, penniless. So she opened a boarding house and he sold apples and newspapers on the streets.

At eighteen he got a job as a clerk on the Mississippi steamer *Knickerbocker*. But the *Knickerbocker* was wrecked on a snag near the mouth of the Ohio. Jim Eads had a bright idea. Why not salvage the hundreds of steamboat wrecks on the bottom of the Mississippi? Soon he and Bill Nelson, his lifelong friend and partner, built a double-hulled boat with derricks, pumps, and a diving bell. They called her the *Submarine.* The insurance companies were glad to pay, and a salvager could have the whole cargo if it had been underwater for five years. Soon Eads and Nelson had a fleet of numbered *Submarines.*

By 1845 he had a wife, all the money he needed, and a fine house on Compton Hill (on Compton and Eads, where the city playground now is). Eads was 41 when the Civil War started. Like "Cump" Sherman, then president of a St. Louis horse-car line, Eads was in favor

of using the Mississippi to split the Confederacy. When the government asked him to build ironclad gunboats, he gladly agreed.

Eads and Nelson put 4000 men to work day and night at the Union Marine Works in Carondelet under the newly invented gas lights. On October 12, 1861, the first ironclad gunboat ever seen slid down the runway at Carondelet. Her name, of course, was the *St. Louis,* and Flag Officer Andrew Hull Foote made her flagship of his river fleet. Up the Tennessee River went Eads's gunboats, to bombard Fort Henry and to force Fort Donelson to surrender to another St. Louisan — U. S. Grant. The gunboats went on to Vicksburg, New Orleans, and Mobile. On the bronze statue of Edward Bates in Forest Park you can see medallions of James Eads and other St. Louisans who helped win the war for the Union.

Gunboat built by James Eads

In 1866 Eads formed the company which was to bridge the Mississippi. The ferryboaters and the steamboaters tried to stop him. But the Baltimore and Ohio Railroad already had puffed into East St. Louis by 1856. Other eastern railroads were bringing their tracks to the Mississippi. The engineers said nobody could build a bridge a third of a mile long. Eads said he could.

Hundreds of men went to work lowering the newly invented cofferdams, or caissons. Into these great chambers they pumped air until they reached bed rock many feet below the bottom of the river. Then they built the piers inside the caissons. Early in 1870 the bridge-builders began to get the "bends." They had to cut the working day to two 45-minute shifts.

When the piers were completed, the steel arches had to be held up by cables until they met in the center of the spans. Eads had to fight Andrew Carnegie to get the kind of steel he needed. Then he had to go to London to raise more money for steel. In the summer heat, the steel tubes expanded so much they would not meet. Eads solved that problem too. He had designed a special pin for just such an emergency.

Section of east pier and caisson

Eads Bridge under construction

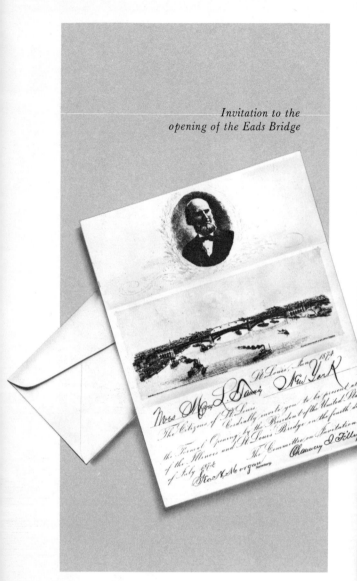

Invitation to the opening of the Eads Bridge

At last, in 1874, the bridge was ready. On opening day, July 4, Eads ran fourteen locomotives onto the bridge. With thousands of visitors looking on, General Sherman drove the last spike. A 100-gun salute was fired. There was a parade several miles long. The bands played, and at night there was a grand fireworks display.

After the bridge was finished, James Eads tackled the problem of keeping the mouth of the Mississippi free of sandbars so the ocean liners could come in to New Orleans. Eads wanted to build jetties, or piers, to force the river to dig out its own 26-foot channel. Again the engineers said he was crazy. But the jetty backers put up the money, and the Mississippi did just what Eads said it would do. The Government paid Eads ten million dollars and gave him a contract to keep the channel open.

Eads did not live to make his last great idea work. The French were trying to promote a canal across Panama to get ships from the Atlantic to the Pacific. Eads wanted to build a marine railway to lift the ships from the Gulf of Mexico and carry them on huge cars to the Pacific. He showed a working model to

bankers in New York. But before he could put his plan into action, he died in New York on March 8, 1887. He is buried in Bellefontaine Cemetery on a bluff overlooking the great river he knew so well. So lived and died this remarkable St. Louisan, James Buchanan Eads, whose skill helped make our city famous throughout the world for one of the finest bridges ever built.

Marine railway
proposed by Eads

Wainwright Building

Louis Sullivan carefully piled book after book on top of the wire bird cage. The cage did not collapse under the heavy weight. He smiled; he now had the answer he was looking for. Sullivan, an architect from Chicago, was interested in the use of steel in designing buildings. From his experiment Sullivan got the idea of basing the structure of a skyscraper on a steel frame. Until this time all buildings had been constructed in layer-cake fashion, with the heaviest materials used on the bottom floor.

Sullivan was hired to come to St. Louis and build several buildings. The most remarkable of these was the Wainwright Building at Seventh and Chestnut, built in 1891. Although it is only ten stories high, it was one of the first real skyscrapers. The idea of the steel structure is still being used in skyscraper construction today. On the Wainwright Building one can see the elaborate decorations which Sullivan was so fond of under the windows on each floor, on the cornice, and on the main entrance.

Of the ten best architectural structures in this country, St. Louis can claim two — one is the Eads Bridge and the other is the Wainwright Building.

Our Place in the Sky

The St. Louis World's Fair of 1904 had come and gone, but people still talked about the balloon races held there. Certain St. Louisans were so enthusiastic about the floating gas-filled bags, that they arranged for the first International Balloon Race to be held in Forest Park in 1907. Balloonists entered from several states and some European countries.

Another St. Louis first was the presidential plane flight that took place at old Kinloch Field when President Theodore Roosevelt had a four-minute spin in a box-styled aircraft with Pilot Archie Hoxie. "I enjoyed every minute of it. By George, it was great," was the way Theodore Roosevelt summed it up. A few years later, St. Louis was selected for the site of the National Air Races because of the great interest in aviation here.

World War I awakened further interest in aviation and speeded its development. New uses were found for flying during the war. After the war, Major Albert Bond Lambert, who had commanded a school for balloon pilots, stimulated flying in St. Louis. From 1920 to 1928 he maintained an airport near Bridgeton at his own expense. Regular airmail got its start during this time when the Robertson Aircraft Company carried mail between St. Louis and Chicago.

One popular flying instructor at Lambert's airport was Minnesota-born Charles A. Lindbergh. Lindbergh — tall, bashful, and slim — made mail runs to Chicago, gave flying lessons, and took part in National Guard activities. Shy though he was, Lindbergh had a love of adventure. When a French aviation enthusiast, Chevalier Raymond Orteig, offered a $25,000 prize to the first pilot who would fly the Atlantic non-stop, Lindbergh accepted the challenge. The only drawback was that Lindbergh had no funds to finance the flight. He went to St. Louis businessmen for money, promising to pay it back if his flight proved successful. The first $1,000 was given by air-minded Major Lambert, and then other St. Louisans, headed by Harold Bixby, President of the Chamber of Commerce, joined in to complete the needed $15,000.

It took months for Lindbergh to get the exact plane he wanted. He had his mind set on the Wright-Bellanca and had almost closed the deal when the company reserved the right to choose the crew. Lindbergh wanted to make the trip alone. As a last resort he went to the Ryan Airlines, Incorporated, in San Diego in February. He found there a group of enthusiastic young engineers and designers. Already newspaper reports from around the globe were

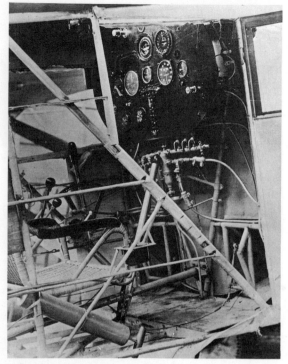

Inside the cockpit of the Spirit of St. Louis

On May 20, 1927, Lindbergh set out with five sandwiches, two canteens of water, and the courage to succeed in flying the Atlantic alone. The plane was loaded with 450 gallons of gasoline. After a slow start he gradually eased his way into the misty sky over Long Island and then moved on toward Nova Scotia. He flew over icebergs, fogs, black ocean, and island mirages. Flying low over the water, he determined the speed and direction of the wind by watching the path of the foam blown from the crest of the ocean whitecaps. The first land he sighted was Ireland; then he saw South England; and at last on May 21, he reached LeBourget Airport in Paris. The "Lone Eagle" had made the trip of 3,610 miles in only 33 hours and 30 minutes.

Lindbergh was a world hero. He returned to the United States the next month, with a trunk-load of medals, scrolls, gifts, and keys heaped on him while abroad. Crowds greeted him in Washington and New York, but the greatest reception of all took place right here on Art Hill in Forest Park. Everyone who could walk, ride, or crawl was out that day to see St. Louis's own hero. Lindbergh, throughout this deluge of praise, gifts, and laurels, kept his modesty, poise, and dignity.

Lindbergh had always disciplined himself,

being printed about other proposed flights. It was necessary to get a good plane — in a hurry. The one who got there first would be the winner. The Ryan Airlines Company said it could build the plane in two months. This meant Lindbergh could start out by the last of May. There was still hope!

Lindbergh needed those two months to map out his flight plan. No detail escaped him. Side by side with Engineer Hall, Lindbergh worked to design the plane. The engine was to be a J-5 Whirlwind, and the cockpit would be in the rear of the plane. They planned to use standard instruments and oversize fuel tanks. They would eliminate any extra weight but put in the very best materials. Lindbergh decided against a parachute in favor of extra fuel. The work went on in San Diego while reports came in of accidents, delays, and tragedies that had befallen most of those who had already started on the non-stop flight.

The Spirit of St. Louis, as Lindbergh named the plane, was finally ready. Lindbergh flew to St. Louis, but there was no time for any ceremonies. He had to use Lambert Field as a refueling station and hurry on to New York.

St. Louis welcomes Lindy

even as a boy in his teens. He said, "I came to the conclusion that if I knew the difference between the right way to do a thing and a wrong way to do it, it was up to me to train myself to do the right thing at all times." Lindbergh's list of good character traits included altruism (interest in others), ambition, brevity, tact, thoroughness, and unselfishness.

The "Lone Eagle" was so grateful to St. Louisans for giving him his start that he permitted his gifts and trophies to be displayed at the Missouri Historical Society. So many people came to see them that he donated them to the Society as well as the thousands of gifts he received later. They are still there for us to see: the flying suit in which he made the trip, the map he used which was mounted on wing

coverings, stockpiles of wristwatches, jewelry, letters, medals, and hundreds of other mementos the public lavished on him. The only thing missing here is the plane, *The Spirit of St. Louis,* which is now in the Smithsonian Institution in Washington, D. C. His greatest tribute to St. Louis was to name his autobiography written years later, *The Spirit of St. Louis.* The book won him the Pulitzer prize.

The success of Lindbergh's flight made St. Louis even more air conscious than before and put it in the foreground of aviation. Lambert Airfield—St. Louis Municipal Airport—has come a long way from that little field from which Lindbergh took off. More and more land was purchased until the airport we go to now as we zoom down Highway 70 stretches over

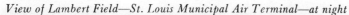

many acres. Lambert is now a major commercial airport, accommodating hundreds of planes flying daily flights from coast to coast. The new Terminal Building, with its spacious, airy architecture, is a must on lists of places to see in this area.

St. Louis has kept pace with the progress in air travel. On the northwest end of the airport is the sprawling McDonnell Aircraft Corporation where some of our nation's space capsules were made. Astronauts come there to meet with engineers and designers before and after an orbital flight to discuss the capsules.

Balloon travel, first airmail run, the first solo transatlantic flight, numerous commercial flights, and space capsules — all make us point with pride to our place in the sky.

MEN! MIGHT! MISSILES!

The boy on the pony hunched his shoulders forward and bent his head low. Almost blinded by the driving rain, he tried to cover his newspapers with his stiff old raincoat. It was no use. The top ones were already soaked.

Well, he was almost finished, anyway. It was after 6:30 A.M., and fourteen-year-old Jim McDonnell had been on his paper route for an hour. He would soon reach the other side of town, where he would turn around and make his way back home for breakfast. Since he had got the pony, he had been able to double the length of his route. He was glad to have the animal for the return trip this morning.

The lightning and thunder got worse. At each crash the little pony threatened to bolt. Then, the brightest flash that Jim had ever seen surrounded him; afterwards, black silence.

When he opened his eyes, he was lying face down in the mud. About fifteen feet to his right, he could see the still body of his pony. The animal had been electrocuted right out from under him.

Jim did not run home in fright. He got up and delivered the few papers that were still dry. The next morning he was up at 5:15 again, getting ready to deliver papers. But now that he had to walk, he went back to his shorter route.

Keeping busy was nothing new to Jim. Since his early childhood he and his brothers had helped out in their dad's old-fashioned general store in Little Rock, Arkansas. Mr. McDonnell was a hard worker himself, and he taught his boys to work hard too.

While Jim was going to high school, he liked

to read about airplanes. Men were finding out how to make better and better planes. Planes were even being used in warfare. Jim made up his mind to learn everything he could about airplanes. When he went away to college in 1917, he told his parents that he would fly back home in his own plane.

His father did not like the idea. He wanted Jim to be a business man, or maybe a doctor or lawyer. At Princeton and later at Massachusetts Institute of Technology, Jim studied how to build and fly airplanes. And when he finished, he really did fly his own plane home. A lot of people came out to the Little Rock airport to see him land. His dad was there too. By this time his father had changed his mind; he was proud of his son. Before long Jim started a company which he named McDonnell and Associates. His idea was to build an airplane that could travel and maneuver faster than any other plane at the time. Jim, of course, was the company's test pilot.

Planes in the 1920's and 1930's were very slow compared with today's jets, but they were still exciting to fly. Their pilots called them "flivvers," because they were often homemade contraptions, put together with odds and ends of machinery. Once when he was flying his own flivver in a contest in New York, Jim found out that all planes were supposed to have lights. Jim's didn't, but he solved the problem by taping a flashlight on each wing tip.

F H Phantom— first jet to fly from a carrier

The next day, while he was putting the plane through some stunts, a part of the tail folded up. Jim stood up and sat on the back of the cockpit, ready to bail out. At the last minute, he slid back into the cockpit and sweated out the landing. The plane was saved. Soon it was repaired and back in the contest.

In 1939 McDonnell started the present company by renting a small office in a building at Lambert-St. Louis Airport. At first the entire staff consisted of just two men. For weeks nobody else in the building even knew that the little company was there. The company grew slowly, but "Mr. Mac," as his workers call him, planned for the future. He was never satisfied; improved planes were always on the drawing boards. When the country needed a new type of plane, the McDonnell company often had one ready. Thus McDonnell's company built the first carrier-based jet fighter for the Navy. It built the world's first twin-engined helicopter, the Whirlaway. McDonnell has been a great leader in space flight also. The company made the Mercury capsule in which our astronauts have orbited the earth. Now it is getting the two-man Gemini capsule ready for its first flight.

First McDonnell office in St. Louis

John F. Kennedy's visit to McDonnell to examine the Gemini Spacecraft—September, 1962

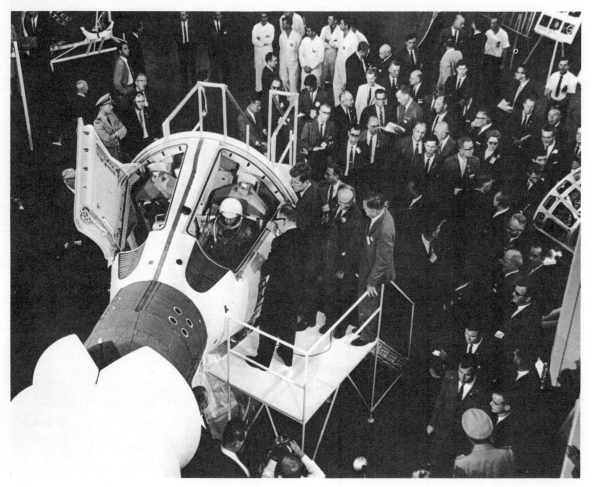

The McDonnell Company is located next to Lambert-St. Louis Air Terminal; it spreads over more than 300 acres. Some of the buildings are assembly plants, where parts of the planes are put together. Some are office buildings, where engineers design new parts or whole new aircraft and spacecraft. There are laboratories and wind tunnels, where parts can be tested. There are special rooms where the engineers can put pilots into conditions like those they will find in space. In one part of the plant there are huge data-processing machines, or electronic brains, to solve difficult mathematical problems.

The McDonnell Aircraft Corporation is Missouri's largest employer. Almost 40,000 people work there. The company is well-known for its policy of hiring all people, regardless of race, and Mr. McDonnell has won a national award for his work in intergroup relations. Mr. Mac has a lot of helpers, but he sets the example for all of them. "Decide which is the most important job to do each day," he says; "then stick with it until it's finished."

McDonnell Aircraft Corporation today

Camp Jackson
May 6, 1861

DAYS OF CONFLICT

A DIVIDED City

Willy Sherman was excited as he walked to Lindell Grove with his father "Cump" and his Uncle Charles. They had trudged all the way to the outskirts of the city to watch the Union soldiers take over Camp Jackson, located at what is now Grand and Laclede. Some rebel Missourians had holed up there, and the Union forces were coming out to make sure no trouble started. Nobody expected any. Willy and his father were mostly interested in watching the marching soldiers.

Suddenly they found themselves ducking flying bullets. Uncle Charles pushed Willy down and fell on top of him. "Cump" then pulled both the boy and his uncle into a gully. The Civil War, which had begun at Fort Sumter on April 12, 1861, had now, a month later, come to St. Louis.

General William T. Sherman

General Ulysses S. Grant

Luckily, neither Willy nor the two men were hit by the bullets. History might have been changed if they had. Willy's father was William Tecumseh Sherman, who later became famous as one of the Union's two best generals. By coincidence, another man who was to be the other outstanding Union General and, later, President of the United States, Ulysses S. Grant, was also in St. Louis on that day. Neither of them had to fight at Camp Jackson — Sherman was president of the Lucas horse-car line in St. Louis, and Grant lived and worked on a farm southwest of St. Louis.

St. Louis played a very important part in the War Between the States, or Civil War. Missouri was a border state between the North and the South. Many of its citizens, including the governor, Claiborne Jackson, felt that the South was right. Most of the Southern sympathizers lived in the rural parts of the state. But in St. Louis most of the people and their

leaders were pro-Union. St. Louis led the fight to keep the whole state in the Union.

Governor Jackson had already called a state convention to try to get Missouri to withdraw from the Union, but failed. When President Lincoln asked for soldiers from Missouri, Jackson refused to send them. Instead, the governor had his friends smuggle guns and ammunition into St. Louis and hide them in Camp Jackson, which was named to honor the governor. Jackson planned to have about 800 men who were gathered at the camp attack the arsenal that stood along the Mississippi River at what is now Second and Arsenal. Only a handful of Union soldiers guarded the arsenal. If the arsenal with all its guns and ammunition fell into Southern hands, the state was certain to join the Confederacy.

While this was going on, St. Louisans were getting ready to defend the city. They held meetings to plan how to keep order if fighting

broke out. One of their leaders was Frank P. Blair, a Republican newspaperman and politician who backed Lincoln. Groups of Irishmen and Germans joined in the planning. All of them were for the Union and against slavery.

The Germans were very active. They held military drills at their Turner Halls (athletic clubs). A crowd of Turners volunteered to defend the arsenal, but the Union general in charge turned them down. He believed there was no danger. The Germans, not to be denied, decided to cross the river to join up in Illinois, but at the last minute Frank Blair got them into the arsenal. At least three of the regimental leaders that marched on Camp Jackson were German—Sigel, Boernstein, and Schuttner. A south St. Louis school is named after Sigel.

Although Blair and others had warned that Jackson's men might attack, the officers did not take the warnings seriously. Finally Captain Nathaniel Lyon took charge of the arsenal,

rising immediately from captain to brigadier-general. He saw to it that plenty of troops were ready to defend it. Working at night, he secretly sent much of the ammunition and weapons to Springfield, Illinois, for safekeeping. When the confederates gathered at Camp Jackson, Lyon disguised himself as a woman and drove right to the camp to spy on it. He then returned to the arsenal and ordered the troops to march out and take over the camp. These were the soldiers that Willy Sherman and his father had come out to watch. Lyon's action saved the arsenal for St. Louis and the Union. More than that, Jefferson Barracks, which was south of the city, was also saved. It had not been a very busy place for several years, but as soon as the war broke out Lincoln sent extra soldiers there. As the war went on, the Barracks became crowded with soldiers. Some received military training there. Others were patients in the post's hospital.

United States Arsenal in St. Louis

After the Camp Jackson incident, Lincoln appointed John C. Fremont to head a special military government in the West. St. Louis was to be its headquarters. Frank Blair thought Fremont would be the great military leader of the war and so recommended him for the job. Fremont was already a hero to many St. Louisans because of his explorations in the West and his conquest of California. But he did not do a good job at St. Louis. When Southern troops advanced to Springfield, Lyon had to meet them with a small force. Fremont failed to send help in time, and Lyon was killed. Fremont finally had to be replaced.

St. Louis was not the scene of mighty battles during the war, but her citizens did some of the hardest and most important work. Some of the leading men and women saw the need for helping wounded soldiers. After some battles the number of wounded men ran into the hundreds and even thousands. There were no hospitals near the battlefields and not enough people to care for the wounded. A group of

James E. Yeatman

St. Louisans volunteered to form the Western Sanitary Commission. This group collected money, ran hospitals, and took care of the wounded in St. Louis and in many other places.

The volunteers got no pay for their work. James Yeatman, a banker, was president of the Commission. Until the end of the war, he spent all of his time directing the Commission. He even moved a bed into his office so that he could stay on duty. (The building which houses Central High School was once called Yeatman High School.) Dr. William Greenleaf Eliot, founder of Washington University, was also a member. He often worked until after midnight. People sometimes saw him walking to his home on the outskirts of town, holding a lantern to light his way. Eliot made several trips to eastern cities and raised thousands of dollars for the Commission.

*Statue of
Nathaniel Lyon
in Lyon Park*

Women formed their own groups to work with the Commission. Two of these groups were the Ladies' Union Aid Society and the Ladies' National League. Mrs. Alfred Clapp, Mrs. T. M. Post, and Mrs. Samuel C. Dorris were officers in the Union Aid Society. These groups made bandages and gathered clothing and food for the wounded soldiers. Other women became nurses. Army officers said that women made better nurses than men. Mrs. Jessie Fremont, wife of John C. Fremont, helped start the Western Sanitary Commission itself.

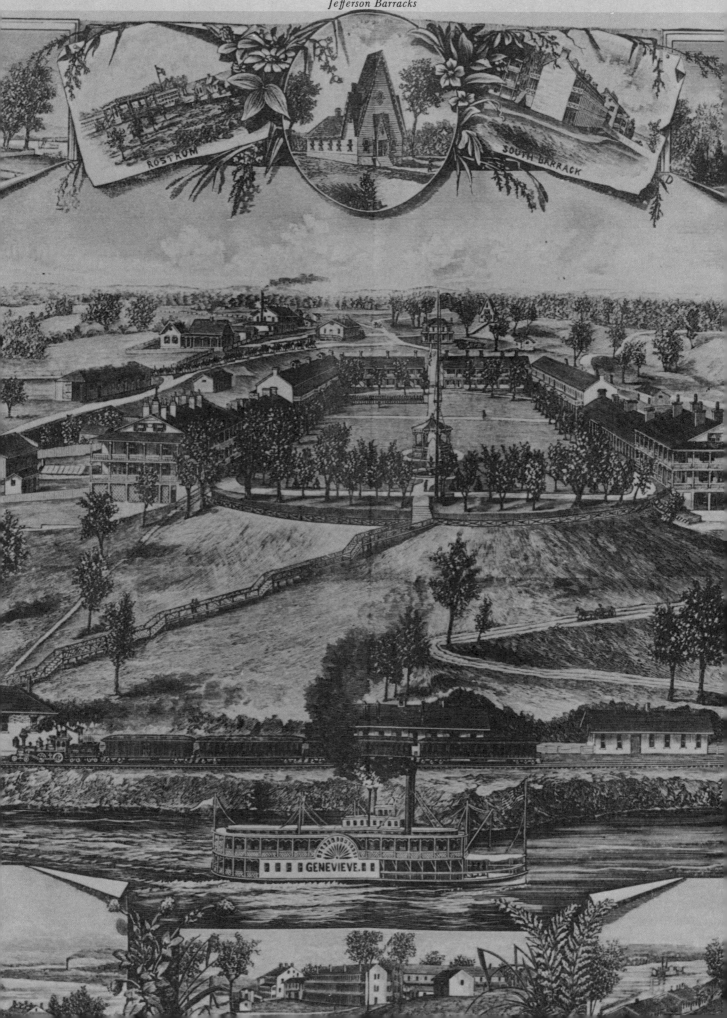

ROSTRUM

SOUTH BARRACK

GENEVIEVE

Civil War military hospital at Broadway and Chestnut

New hospitals were built by the government, and other buildings were changed into hospitals to care for the hundreds of wounded coming in from the South. St. Louis hospitals treated more than 60,000 patients. The Commission had to find people to work in these hospitals and in hospitals in eight other states and the Indian territory! In addition to equipping hospitals, the Commission provided convalescent homes—for soldiers who were not seriously wounded or ill but who needed long periods to recover. It also built soldiers' homes for men stopping in St. Louis on their way home from the fighting.

Civilian refugees needed help too. Confederate soldiers ran pro-Union Missourians out of their homes in the southern part of the state. These people often fled to St. Louis. The Commission provided refuge homes for them. Many freed Negroes were left homeless, penniless, and sick. The Commission improved the camps that they lived in, gave them medicine, food, and clothing, and helped them find jobs.

To speed up the movement of wounded soldiers, the Commission took over two railroad cars. They put in berths and cooking equipment and supplied nurses. These were probably the first hospital cars made in the United States. In 1862 the Commission helped the government outfit the first "floating hospital." As the war went on, steamboats were used to move thousands of wounded soldiers quickly and safely to hospitals far from the battlefield.

The Civil War had a terrible effect on Missouri and, particularly, St. Louis. Boys who had grown up together and even brothers took opposite sides and fought against each other. Death and destruction struck people of both sides as the war raged back and forth across the state. For its population Missouri supplied about as many soldiers as any state in the Union. Missouri casualties were also high, but without the work of the Western Sanitary Commission thousands more would have died than actually did.

Major General Sterling Price of St. Louis, Confederate Army officer who defeated General Lyon's forces at Springfield.

De Menil House

One of the houses saved from the "headache ball" and the giant claws of wrecking machines is the DeMenil House at Thirteenth and Cherokee. This elegant house, with its ornamental Ionic columns and cast-iron balconies, started out as a small seven-room cottage.

The cottage was built in 1842 by Henri Chatillon. He was a well-known guide to the West and owned a popular saloon on the riverfront. In 1856 Chatillon sold his home and the surrounding nine acres to Dr. Nicholas De-Menil, who wanted it as a country place.

Dr. DeMenil, a French physician, had made a fortune through part ownership in the first successful chain of retail drug stores in St. Louis. His wife was the former Emilie Sophie Chouteau, daughter of Colonel Auguste P. Chouteau. The DeMenils continued to live in the older part of the city until 1863. At that time they added a nine-room section to the front of Chatillon's cottage. This front section was much more elaborate than the older part. The ceilings were much higher, and it was

grander in every way. The tall columns and the decorative balconies reminded them of beautiful southern mansions.

During these Civil War years St. Louis was under military law, and the southern families were watched very closely. Therefore, the De-Menils moved to their country home; still uneasy, they placed iron bars on all of the first-floor windows.

Dr. DeMenil died in 1882, and his son Alexander inherited the property. The DeMenil family kept it until 1945, when it was sold to Lee Hess. In 1961 Hess sold the property to the Missouri State Highway Commission to make way for Interstate Highway 44. Interested citizens heard about the sale and decided to try to save the house. When the Highway Department chose an alternate route for the new highway, by-passing the DeMenil Home, Union Electric Company bought the house. This company presented it to the Landmarks Association, which is restoring it as it was in the late 1800's, an "elegant" mansion.

During Leisure Time

Boating party
viewing Central Cascades
at the Louisiana
Purchase Exposition

A Garden Grows

The long trip up the river was over and the steamboat, *Maid of Orleans,* was finally tied up at the levee in St. Louis. A young passenger, Henry Shaw, unloaded a few pieces of hardware, and then rented a small, second floor room on Main Street, north of Market Street. In this room he slept, cooked his own meals, and started his hardware business in 1819.

Shaw worked so hard at this business that by 1839 he had earned a quarter of a million dollars. He found in that year alone he had made $25,000, mostly in outfitting fur traders. Wisely, Shaw noted that this was "more money than a man in my circumstances ought to make in a single year." So he sold his business and retired.

In the first few years of retirement Shaw made several trips to England. On one of these trips he saw for the first time the beautiful flower gardens around one of the palaces. Shaw returned to St. Louis with the conviction that the people of St. Louis should have a chance to see such beauty too. During the next several years Shaw considered how he could get such a garden for this city. His good friend, Dr. George Engelmann, tried to convince him that

Henry Shaw

Shaw's city home

he should develop a real botanical garden — a garden in which there would be collections of different kinds of plants and a place for studying and teaching about them. Henry Shaw respected Dr. Engelmann as a doctor, but he was not quite ready to take his advice as a botanist. It took another man to convince Shaw that the botanical garden was what he wanted. This was Sir Joseph Hooker, director of the Royal Botanical Garden at Kew, England. When Sir Joseph came to America on a trip, he stayed in St. Louis as the house guest of Henry Shaw. Their talks helped Shaw see the importance of a good botanical garden in this part of the country.

Shaw owned the seventy-five acres around his country home. This was the land he used for the garden. In 1859 he built a brick and stone library which he filled with books about plants. Later came greenhouses and for them were gathered plants from all over the world. In 1860 the garden was ready to be opened to the public. Shaw himself named it the Missouri Botanical Garden. But St. Louisans have from the first fondly called it Shaw's Garden.

For thirty years Shaw kept all of the ac-

counts, made the plans, and hired the workmen. In his own neat handwriting he recorded the names of his gardeners as well as the days and hours they worked. All of these records and his personal belongings are found today in Shaw's country home in the Garden.

As you look at this country home you will see the tower from which Shaw looked at his beautiful garden. From this tower you can also see a grove of sassafras trees. It was for the tower and the grove that he named his country home Tower Grove. Shaw owned a house in the city too. It was on the southwest corner of Seventh and Locust streets, where the Katz Drug Store is today. In fair weather he rode from one home to the other on a narrow winding path.

Shaw's Garden is not the only large gift of land Shaw made to St. Louis. In 1870 he gave the city the park next to the Garden named after his country house — Tower Grove. It is bounded by Grand and Kingshighway, Magnolia and Arsenal. You may have seen the open air bandstand in the park. Mr. Shaw was not a musician himself, but he enjoyed listening to the music played there on Sunday after-

Shaw's country home

Climatron

*Sculptured likeness of Henry Shaw
in the Garden Mausoleum*

noons. Tower Grove Park is still a popular meeting place for many people in St. Louis who want to play tennis, ride bikes, or just enjoy the park.

Henry Shaw continued to be active in the affairs of the city. He was one of the city's leading citizens until his death from malaria in 1889. He was laid to rest in the Mausoleum long prepared in the midst of the Garden he created.

After Shaw's death the town house was moved brick by brick to the Garden according to the directions in his will. You can still see the Shaw town house behind the stone walls on Tower Grove Avenue. In recent years other interesting sights have been added to the gardens. The newest building is the Climatron. It is the world's first controlled-climate greenhouse. In other buildings there are flower shows from time to time. There is a plan for a walking tour which leads one past forty different kinds of trees marked for identification. All of these things were made possible by Henry Shaw to whom many people still pay tribute by visiting his mausoleum before they leave the Garden.

His Mysterious Majesty

On a March evening in 1878 a dozen leading St. Louisans met in the luxurious Lindell Hotel on Sixth and Washington. They had been invited to dinner by Charles Slayback, a wealthy grain dealer. They were told only that the meeting would be to promote the business interests of St. Louis.

Mr. Slayback and his brother, Alonzo, a former colonel in the Confederate Army, had an idea. They proposed that St. Louis have a grand ball and a parade like the Mardi Gras Carnival in New Orleans. It was to be organized by a society called "The Mysterious Order of the Veiled Prophet."

Colonel Alonzo Slayback had borrowed the idea of the Veiled Prophet from a then popular poem by the Irish poet Thomas Moore. The poem, "Lalla Roohk," told of an eighth-century rebel leader in Khorassan, a province in ancient Persia. He was known to his followers as the Great Mohanna, or the Veiled One. This original Veiled Prophet had lost an eye and part of his nose in one of many battles. Turning his handicap into an advantage, the Great Mohanna wore a veil of silver gauze and invented the tale that he was a heaven-sent prophet whose face was so bright it would harm people who looked at it. Colonel Slayback liked the air of mystery around a *veiled* prophet from far off Khorassan, but our Veiled Prophet was to be a good man, a kind of Santa Claus for grown-ups.

The news of his first visit brought families from miles around riding in horse-drawn farm wagons to the city. Special trains ran to St. Louis and visitors took advantage of reduced fares. Out of the old Union Depot at Twelfth Boulevard and Clark Street (where Police Headquarters now stands) poured thousands and thousands of visitors. Steamboats eased up to the levee with thousands more. Many walked. It was the show of a lifetime—too big to be missed.

As many as 50,000 visitors nudged elbows cheerfully with each other, ate the restaurants out of food, and occupied every available sleeping spot. On the night of the parade many of them could be seen waving five- or ten-dollar bills trying to get a choice viewing place. The crowd was so great around the den where the floats were kept that Police Chief McDonough and his twenty-four mounted officers could not clear a path. Finally, the crowd moved just enough. In a burst of torchlight, as whistling torpedoes signaled the start, the first floats appeared. Each was drawn by six horses and accompanied by twenty torch bearers. Bumping and creaking, the parade moved over cobblestone streets, north on Twelfth to Washington Avenue and then east to the foot of James B. Eads's wonderful new bridge.

For children and parents alike the parade was a trip into a land of fantasy and magic. Outlandish scenes with dangerous monsters, brave heroes, and beautiful maidens rolled by. On the last float was the Veiled Prophet himself. Splendidly dressed and carrying in his hand the magic mirror which showed the past, present, and future, the Veiled Prophet struck awe in every man, woman, and child along the parade route.

Everyone had a roaring good time that night of Tuesday, October 8, 1878, gazing goggle-eyed at this strange and beautiful spectacle. Nothing like it had ever been seen here before. As the city was much smaller then than now, it was a challenge to those along the parade route to discover who the masked men were. By heckling the men on the floats, the bystanders could often tell their identity through their reactions.

Even mishaps could not spoil these early parades. Japanese lanterns sometimes caught fire and fell into the crowd. (But little boys had great sport stamping out the fire.) In one parade the city marshal had his hair set afire by a carelessly handled torch. In another an awning collapsed under the weight of fifty spectators. But things like this were expected from time to time.

The early custom of the Veiled Prophet was to arrive on the levee in a highly decorated floating barge. This was discontinued after costumes of the royal party were ruined one year by a sudden belching of smoke from a nearby

Veiled Prophet Parade of 1887

*Hester Bates Laughlin—
first crowned Veiled Prophet Queen*

*A recent queen being crowned
by the Veiled Prophet*

Veiled Prophet Ball of today

Queen's float in the parade

boat. Now the Prophet makes his first appearance at the ball.

The lighting effects for the parades were very elaborate. "Grand illuminations" were popular in the seventies. Huge arches of gas jets inside colored globes spanned the main thoroughfares at intervals from Twelfth to Fourth streets. Sidewalk lamp posts were made into brilliant "trees of light," each made up of twenty-five clustered globes of varying colors.

The store fronts were gay with flags and bunting and their own arrangements of lights and lanterns. Inside, the stores were brightly lighted and display advertisements in the newspapers assured that "strangers are welcome."

The Veiled Prophet Ball followed the parade. At first the ball was held at the Merchants' Exchange Building, 111 North Third Street. Later, the Coliseum at Washington and Jefferson avenues was used. In 1936 the ball moved to Kiel Auditorium.

Young women who attended the early balls remembered the long waits while the men, after riding on the floats, changed their costumes for formal dress and arrived late. In the twenties the ball was held the night after the parade, allowing the members of the Order of the Veiled Prophet to be better hosts to the young women attending.

In the beginning of his reign the Veiled Prophet had no formal coronation of a queen. Instead he selected a young woman for the first

dance. She was called the "belle of the ball." The first was Miss Suzie Slayback, Colonel Slayback's niece. The wife of the President of the United States, Mrs. Grover Cleveland, received the same honor a few years later.

In 1894 Miss Hester Bates Laughlin was officially crowned Queen of Love and Beauty. Since that time, except during the two world wars, St. Louis society has had a new queen each October.

In recent years the Queen of Love and Beauty with her four special Maids of Honor has occupied a special float in the parade. The Queen carries a bouquet of hundreds of rare orchids from Shaw's Garden.

From 1878 to the present is a long time. Yet each year the Veiled Prophet appears as vigorous as ever. He seems to enjoy our modern St. Louis as much as he did the old one. His floats now roll over seven miles of smoothly paved streets instead of the bumpy one and a half miles of an earlier era. Electricity has taken the place of torches, and tractors are used instead of horses. Perhaps the floats are more lavish now than before. But one thing is certain. The g r e e t i n g of thousands of St. Louisans for the Veiled Prophet is as affectionate as ever.

Festival Hall and Central Cascades

MEET ME AT THE FAIR

On April 30, 1904, President Theodore Roosevelt touched an electric key in the White House. Eight hundred miles away — in Forest Park, St. Louis — 10,000 flags unfurled, machinery whirred, waterfalls tumbled downhill, and bands burst into music. So began a seven-month celebration to which the whole world was invited — the Louisiana Purchase Exposition, usually known as the St. Louis World's Fair.

For many years St. Louis had been getting ready for this celebration. David Rowland Francis, former mayor of St. Louis and Governor of Missouri, had for a long time had the ambition to bring a world's fair to St. Louis. Pierre C h o u t e a u, great-great-nephew of Auguste, suggested the date — 1903, the hundredth anniversary of the Louisiana Purchase. The President of the United States asked all the countries of the world to send people and exhibits. Because all this took time, the date for the opening was changed to 1904.

For the fairgrounds, the city loaned the western half of Forest Park. Washington University, then at Washington Avenue and Nineteenth Street, leased its new grounds west of present Skinker Boulevard. Other land came from private owners.

Led by Francis and Chouteau, the newly formed Louisiana Purchase Exposition Company planned buildings and exhibits. To pay the many bills, they talked the city, state, and federal governments into giving $10,000,000. From willing St. Louisans they collected $5,000,000 more.

On December 20, 1901, in frozen, snow-covered Forest Park, a small army of workmen began a three-year job. They chopped down trees, paved streets, and dug lagoons. They boxed in the River Des Peres, a crooked little stream that wandered all over the fairgrounds. They set up hundreds of statues, and they built many palaces. Most of the buildings were meant to last only as long as the Fair.

With the work of building well on its way, St. Louisans had time to worry about their city's water. They were used to its pale chocolate color and muddy taste. But thousands of visitors were coming to St. Louis. All over the country people were humming, singing, or whistling "Meet me in St. Louis, Louis. Meet me at the Fair." For the visitors and for the Fair's lagoons and waterfalls, the city's leaders wanted clean, pure water. The mud had to go, and it went, for Mayor Rolla Wells saw to that. He and Commissioner Ben Adkins tried scheme after scheme. Finally in March, 1904, under the direction of engineer John F. Wixford, St. Louis water had lost its grittiness and was as clear as crystal. St. Louis was ready for its guests.

Opening day came and so did almost 200,000 people, most of them on street cars.

Clanging through the open country west of Union Boulevard, the cars pulled up at the Fair's entrance. The Jefferson Memorial stands there today. Before going in, most of the people lined up along Administration Avenue, now Lindell Boulevard. There they watched a parade. Then the watchers crowded after the marchers into the fairgrounds.

At the foot of a monument to the Louisiana Purchase, John Philip Sousa's band played a concert. A chorus sang "Hymn to the West," a song written especially for the Fair. William Howard Taft, who was United States Secretary of War, made a speech. So did the President of the World's Fair, David R. Francis. The Louisiana Purchase Exposition had begun.

Wide-eyed crowds jammed the fairgrounds in the months that followed. There was much to see and hear. At the top of Art Hill was the Palace of Art, the only building meant to last. It is now the central part of our Art Museum. The works of art inside had come from nineteen countries besides the United States. In front of the Palace of Art was Festival Hall, which contained the world's biggest organ. Artificial waterfalls raced down the hill in front of the Hall and splashed into the Grand Basin. Italian boatmen sang as they steered their gondolas through the Basin and the park's lagoons.

Most of the forty-three states then in the Union had a building apiece on the fairgrounds. Missouri's, naturally, was the biggest and finest.

Louisiana Purchase Monument and Palace of Varied Industries

Many important social gatherings were held there, where the guests could enjoy them in comfort. Unlike most of the buildings, this one was warmed by steam heat when the weather was chilly and cooled by cold air when the weather was hot.

The Palaces in the park had many interesting exhibits. The wireless telegraph in the Palace of Electricity drew a crowd. The visitors watched the operator send a message all the way to Chicago. They could listen in on a machine to the sound that he made.

In the Agricultural Building cows were milked twice a day. Visitors stopped also to look at a statue of President Roosevelt carved out of butter and a bear made of prunes.

The Transportation Building was a popular spot, with its old locomotives and its small railway that carried passengers over four miles of track.

In the Palace of Education were wax figures from a German medical school, each showing a different kind of disease. There, too, public school children read and wrote and did arithmetic, while their teacher showed the public the latest and best ways of teaching.

Many of the exhibits in the different palaces moved under their own power. A giant loom wove handkerchiefs. Machines made clay into pottery. Soap bubbles floated out of one of the many fountains, while perfume — free to anyone who wanted it — bubbled out of others.

There was no zoo in the park then, but sightseers could see figures of animals in an exhibit that started with the ancient dinosaur and included the modern whale. Hundreds of live birds from all parts of the world made their homes in the biggest cage ever built.

For those who were interested in dwellings there were copies of castles from Germany, France, China, and many other countries. Humble homes were among them — the cabin of Abraham Lincoln, a Swedish farmhouse, the log house of General Grant, the ranch home used by Theodore Roosevelt when he was building up his health out west.

On the land west of Forest Park were other kinds of homes. The people who lived in them were strange and interesting to St. Louisans. Among them were tall Patagonians from South America, perspiring Eskimos in heavy furs and parkas, seventy tribes of Indians living in tepees, polite hairy Ainus — the earliest natives of Japan — and the smallest people at the Fair — the African Negritos. The Negritos were very skillful with the bow and arrow. Shortly after the Fair opened, sparrows swarmed over the fairgrounds. The officials sent the Negritos out to get rid of some of the troublesome birds. They did the job gladly and quickly.

Of all these peoples, the most interesting to World's Fair visitors were the natives of the Philippine Islands. Over a thousand of them camped on a great piece of land that is now

David R. Francis opening the Fair

Palace of Art

Wydown Terrace. They included people in all stages of civilization, low and high. The largest crowd of watchers peered at a tribe of head hunters, the Igorotes. Their up-to-date chief insisted on having a telephone in his hut. On their fenced-in land the natives raised their own rice. They ate it with the most important food on their menu — dog meat. Getting dogs for the Igorotes was a problem. St. Louisans did not want even stray animals to end up in a cooking pot. But the visitors had to be fed, and so the dogs were provided.

Another popular part of the Fair was the amusement section — the Pike. It was on the land north of Lindell, between DeBaliviere and Skinker. The many foreign restaurants there served food that most Americans had never eaten before. But some American food at the Fair was different too. In 1904 St. Louisans and their guests bit into their first hot dogs, licked ice cream cones for the first time, and learned to like a new drink — iced tea.

Visitors wandering through the Pike listened to yodelers in a beautiful village called the Tyrolean Alps. Important guests stayed in its great hotel and ate in its big restaurant. In Mysterious Asia the sightseers saw Turkish swordsmen. For fifteen cents they could ride camels through the streets of Cairo. If that was too expensive, they could ride on donkeys for a dime. At Hagenbeck's Circus they watched elephants go down slides into pools of water.

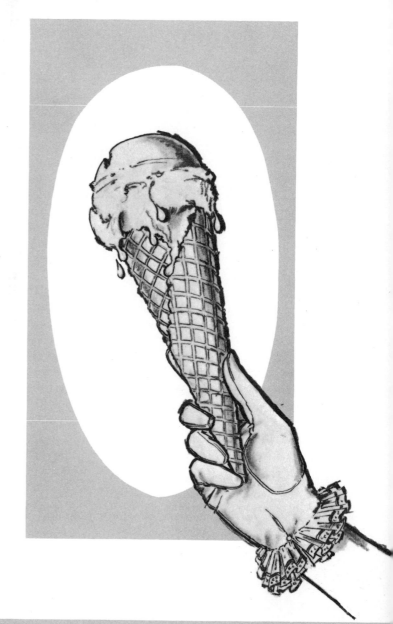

Missouri State Building

In the Irish village they saw lace being made and listened to a singer who afterwards became famous — John McCormack. In the village called Early St. Louis they got to know a friendly cowboy who swung a lariat. You may have heard of him. His name was — Will Rogers.

Crossing the street to Forest Park, the crowds found other amusements. There they rode on a giant Ferris or Observation Wheel that could carry two thousand people. The Observation Wheel was a good place to stay away from during a thunderstorm. When lightning stopped the electricity, riders got a longer turn than they wanted, but they spent the extra time perched high above the ground.

Not far away there was a battle to watch. Some time before, the Dutch settlers in South Africa had lost a war to the British South Africans. Twice each day soldiers who had been in that war refought one if its battles — and twice each day the British won.

There were contests to watch too. For a $100,000 prize many men tried to make a successful flight in an airship. Some of them were not even able to get their planes off the ground. Others quickly crashed. Finally, in October, one of the fliers managed to rise two-thousand feet and fly for thirty-seven minutes — the first such flight in history. The first controlled balloon flight was also made on the fairgrounds.

House of Tinguianes in the Philippine Reservation

General Grant's log cabin. Ulysses S. Grant lived in this house south of St. Louis before becoming leader of the Union Army.

Crowds at the Fair grew bigger during the summer. St. Louis homes were packed with relatives and friends from out of town. The city's hotels were filled too, especially a new one built just for the Fair. It was called the Outside Inn, because it was just outside the grounds and b e c a u s e the one inside the grounds was called Inside Inn.

For St. Louis school children, that summer was a time to remember. Many of them arrived early each morning with their lunches in paper bags. In the evening they often met their parents at the gate, ate a box supper while they listened to a band or orchestra, and watched 300,000 lights go on at sundown. When school started again, class after class came to the Fair with their teachers.

Almost every day at the Fair had its own name and special celebration. There were Missouri Day, Indian Territory Day, American Boy Day, and many others. On a cold November 26, President Roosevelt came to the Fair for the day in his honor — President's Day. Many people, bundled up in furs and winter coats, turned out to welcome him. With true Teddy Roosevelt energy, he enjoyed every minute of his visit.

On the closing day, December 1, 1904, St Louis honored David R. Francis, the man who worked for five years to make the Fair a success. Over 200,000 people watched him re-

Village of the Tyrolean Alps

ceive a gift from a grateful city — a silver tea service worth $17,000. At midnight the President of the World's Fair climbed to the speaker's platform of the Louisiana Monument, which was decorated from top to bottom with lights. Raising both hands toward the buildings, he said, "Farewell, a long farewell to all thy greatness." The band played "Auld Lang Syne." Fireworks spelled out the words "Farewell" and "Good Night." The Fair was over.

Before long, workmen were back in Forest Park again, taking down buildings and carting away exhibits. Soon nothing was left of the Fair except the Art Museum, the Bird Cage, the Grand Basin, the lagoons, and some Washington University buildings. You can see them all today.

The Fair left other memories. Shortly after it closed, the St. Louis Board of Education voted to spend $1,000 for mounted animals, models of flowers, art objects, and other articles from the exhibits. Several foreign countries donated some of their material. In 1905 the newly created "Educational Museum" began lending and delivering these articles to the schools. Today that museum is still operating as the St. Louis Public Schools Division of Audio-Visual Education. Every week its trucks bring films, filmstrips, recordings, and pictures to the city's schools. A set of World's Fair prints is listed in its catalog. Among them is a good map of the exposition grounds.

The Louisiana Purchase Exposition Company had planned carefully. When the great celebration was over, it owed not a cent — in fact, there was money left over. Later, when the materials from the torn down buildings were sold, a large sum of money was on hand. From the very beginning, the Missouri Historical Society had helped greatly in making the fair a success. It was only just that the money should be used in its behalf. Today, in Forest Park — at the former entrance of the Fair — you can see the statue of Thomas Jefferson in the Jefferson Memorial, home of the Missouri Historical Society. The statue of St. Louis on the top of Art Hill was also bought with money from the Fair and presented by Mr. Francis to the city in gratitude for the cooperation of officials and citizens.

Today, through books, pictures, and films, St. Louisans still relive with pride the event that stamped their city's name on the map of the world — the St. Louis World's Fair.

Bird Cage

Exhibits of the St. Louis Public Schools in the Palace of Education

OLYMPIC GAMES ST. LOUIS 1904

St. Louis was the scene of the first Olympic games held in the United States. They were held from August 29 to September 3, 1904, at Francis Field, now Washington University's football stadium.

Only a few nations sent representatives: Germany, Greece, Hungary, Ireland, Australia, Cuba, the Philippines, and the South African Republic. The Americans won most of the events, capturing twenty-one of the twenty-two track and field contests.

The big event was the marathon race, over a route of about twenty-four miles of road. Thirty-one runners entered the race on that hot, sultry day. They were allowed but one water stop, and that was about twelve miles out. Only fourteen finished. The winner, Thomas J. Hicks, was given sponge-downs along the way with warm water from the tank of an automobile. As he staggered across the finish line, a band played, and Alice, the daughter of President Roosevelt, presented him with a bouquet of roses.

The 1904 Olympic games were the third held in modern times. The games had originated in Greece fourteen centuries earlier. The first modern Olympics were held in Athens in 1896; the second, in Paris in 1900. These Olympics were the forerunners of today's huge Olympic Games.

Thomas Hicks, winner of the marathon race

124

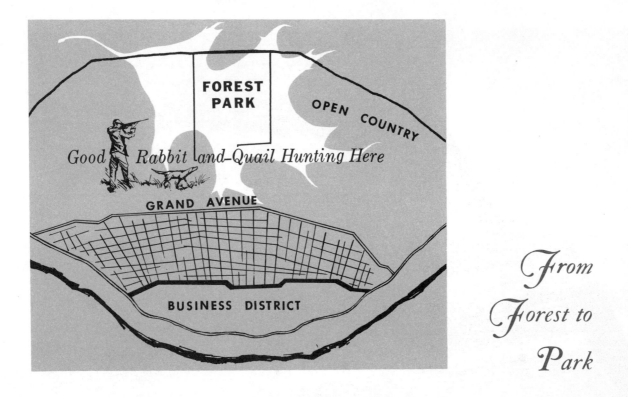

Good *Rabbit and-Quail Hunting Here*

FOREST PARK

OPEN COUNTRY

GRAND AVENUE

BUSINESS DISTRICT

From Forest to Park

T he struggle to establish Forest Park was carried on for four years. From 1870 to 1874, Hiram Leffingwell, a real estate man, led the battle. He wanted the city to buy 2754 acres of land about a mile west of the city limits (Grand Avenue, then) for a park. The people of St. Louis didn't want to do it. Some of them thought it was too far away from the city. Others thought the land should be used for truck farms. Still others claimed they didn't need a *forest* park when there was so much forest around the city anyway.

But Leffingwell wasn't discouraged. Finally, in 1874, after the area had been reduced to 1374 acres, the city bought the land and appointed a Board of Commissioners to administer the park. Improvements were made. Roadways and rustic bridges were built. One old abandoned building was converted into a refreshment stand. Another one was made into offices for the engineers. The board also worked to get roads and streetcars to the park. By 1876 the new park was ready for dedication. People came by carriages, special trains, and on foot to have a part in this ceremony. They were already showing pride in their new possession.

This pride is still alive today as we share "our park" with people from all over the world. On a single trip to Forest Park, visitors can catch a glimpse of many facets of St. Louis life. For the sports fan our park offers tennis, golf, skating, fishing, boating, baseball, and many other team sports. For the culturally minded we have the Art Museum and the Municipal Opera. For the lover of natural beauty, the Jewel Box, outdoor formal gardens, and natural forested areas are a delight. Students surely enjoy the Planetarium, the Missouri Historical Society Museum, and the Zoological Garden. Most of these attractions have their own interesting histories. Here are a few . . . .

DEDICATED TO ART AND FREE TO ALL· MDCDIII

126

Our first art museum was called the St. Louis Museum of Fine Arts and was housed in a beautiful building at Nineteenth and Locust. Built in 1881, it was the gift of Wayman Crow, co-founder of Washington University. For twenty-five years it was both our city museum and a department of Washington University. During this period its collections grew steadily.

In 1900 the city granted the museum directors the right to erect a new building in Forest Park. They had just chosen a beautiful site when the Art Commission of the World's Fair Company approached them, looking for a place to house its displays. The Commission agreed to build at the site already chosen. From the beginning, it was also agreed that the center part of the Palace of Art would be a permanent structure. It was to be our City Art Museum after the Fair was closed in 1904. Bedford gray limestone and Roman brick were chosen as the materials to be used in this fireproof center section.

During the Fair nineteen countries were assigned exhibit space on the ground floor. Several rooms on the second floor were used for late entries. With the exception of some paintings of historical importance in the American section, the World's Fair collection was made up of modern works. This was one of the finest showings of art ever assembled in the world.

In 1906 the collections of our first museum were transferred to the new building, which had been given to the city by the World's Fair Company. The bronze tablet marking the dedication of the St. Louis Museum of Fine Arts, the first museum west of the Mississippi, was placed in the lobby of the present Art Museum, where it can be seen today.

At first the museum was supported by memberships, by a special contribution from Washington University, and by donations from friends. But in 1907 the people of St. Louis voted a tax to support it. Although the museum still receives many gifts from generous friends, its largest income is from this city tax, paid by the citizen of St. Louis.

In the museum are many different kinds of paintings. You are almost sure to find some pictures you will like very much. The sculpture includes classic as well as modern masterpieces. There are collections of textiles, furniture, and ceramics. There are "period rooms" showing the interiors of beautiful old English, Early American, or French homes. There is an Egyptian collection with a mummy as one of the main items of interest.

Although many of these collections are permanent, the Art Museum does have temporary displays of special artists and masterpieces from time to time.

The art on the outside of the building itself is very fine too. On each side of the main entrance is a large figure. The one on the left as you enter represents "Painting," and that on the right represents "Sculpture." Above the six Corinthian columns at the entrance are six statues symbolizing different periods of art. Around the outer walls are twenty-two stone medallions or portraits of the most famous artists in the history of the world. Such men as Michelangelo, Dürer, da Vinci, Rembrandt, and Velazquez are included.

From the first museum of 1881 and the collections borrowed from other countries in 1904, our Art Museum has grown to include more than 700,000 works. Forty centuries of skill and genius from all parts of the world are represented within its walls.

Missouri
Historical
Society

About the time that St. Louis was 100 years old some St. Louisans began to worry about historical materials that were quickly disappearing. So in 1866 a few leading citizens met at the Old Courthouse to form a society that would be responsible for saving everything of historical value.

You will probably recognize the names of some of the men who were at that first meeting, for schools were named after Elihu Shepard, Henry Shaw, William Greenleaf Eliot, and Edward Bates. These men and their friends met in different offices around town to hear talks on historical subjects. A basement room in the Old Courthouse was used as a library and museum for the things the Society collected. At first the collection was mostly Indian relics from the mounds, which were being destroyed. The Society enlarged the collection by advertising in the newspapers for souvenirs and other interesting objects the people might have. You can still see some of the things donated years ago.

By 1886 the collection had outgrown the room in the courthouse. So the Society raised money to buy an old home on the corner of Sixteenth and Locust streets. The Society used that building for many years as a meeting place as well as a museum and library.

When the World's Fair of 1904 closed, there was quite a bit of money left over, so the Fair Company built a memorial building in Forest Park where the entrance to the Fair had been, at DeBaliviere near Lindell Boulevard. It was a memorial to President Thomas Jefferson, who had

Statue of Thomas Jefferson

Steamboat Room

arranged the Louisiana Purchase. Because the Missouri Historical Society had helped so much in gathering information and materials for the World's Fair, the Society was given the use of the Jefferson Memorial as a permanent home. The Society has occupied this building since 1913.

From the beginning Jefferson Memorial has been a public museum as well as a place for study and research. In the museum you may see hundreds of thousands of items. The personal belongings of Lewis and Clark, weapons used by the early explorers, medical and surgical tools used in the early days, pictures of the Veiled Prophet queens, old fire fighting equipment, steamboat mementos, Charles Lindbergh's trophies and gifts, and many, many more items of interest are displayed. The Society's library has nearly 100,000 volumes. It has the paper that was signed when the United States took over the Louisiana Territory, clippings of historical events, and pictures of every decade of St. Louis history.

The Missouri Historical Society has always been supported by donations and memberships in the Society. A few years ago some of the women members opened a Country Store in the west wing of the building. Here you can buy small gifts. Profit from the store goes to the Society.

Not only does the Missouri Historical Society make sure that the history of St. Louis is not lost — but it also provides an interesting way to learn about that history.

Zoo

The Zoo began in 1909 as a dream of George Dieckmann. He was watching girls and boys laughing at eight monkeys left over from the 1904 World's Fair. Dieckmann decided right then to start a zoo. He found that the newspapers and the St. Louis Zoological Society were really interested. But they couldn't solve the problem of where to keep the animals. Dieckmann stirred up public interest in his project. He brought several bear cubs from the west coast and showed them on the corner of West Pine and Euclid. Later he suggested keeping animals in Forest Park. Although many people thought it was a great idea, nothing was done about it until after Henry Kiel became mayor in 1912. Kiel gave the zoo a real boost. Under his leadership, the city passed an ordinance setting aside 77 acres in Forest Park for a zoo.

Dieckmann had another idea. Since the zoo was really for the children, why not let them buy their own elephant? They could bring pennies and nickels; no one was permitted to contribute more than a nickel. It did not take long to raise the $2385 needed. Miss Jim, as the elephant was named, spent her first two nights in St. Louis in a garage at 4564 West Pine. On the day that she was to go to the park, 3000 school children gathered to watch Mayor Kiel ride Miss Jim to her new home. A 75-piece band led the way. During the year the citizens voted overwhelmingly to be taxed for building a zoo.

As far as possible, the zoo was to be cageless. The animals were to have homes as natural as they could be. This idea was so well carried out that we have one of the most interesting zoos in the world.

Although there are over two thousand creatures making their home in our zoo today, a few have stood out as favorites. Miss Jim was very popular for the thirty-two years she lived. During that time she gave rides to 300,000 children. Blondie, the python, which had to be force-fed because of paralyzed jaw muscles, always attracted quite a crowd at her monthly feedings. Two other popular animals were Happy and Pao Pei, the giant pandas. They tumbled and sloshed in the zoo pools for their delighted audiences. Phil, probably the largest gorilla ever reared in a zoo, was playful and good-natured most of the time. He would pretend to be asleep in a pool of water when a crowd gathered close

Miss Jim

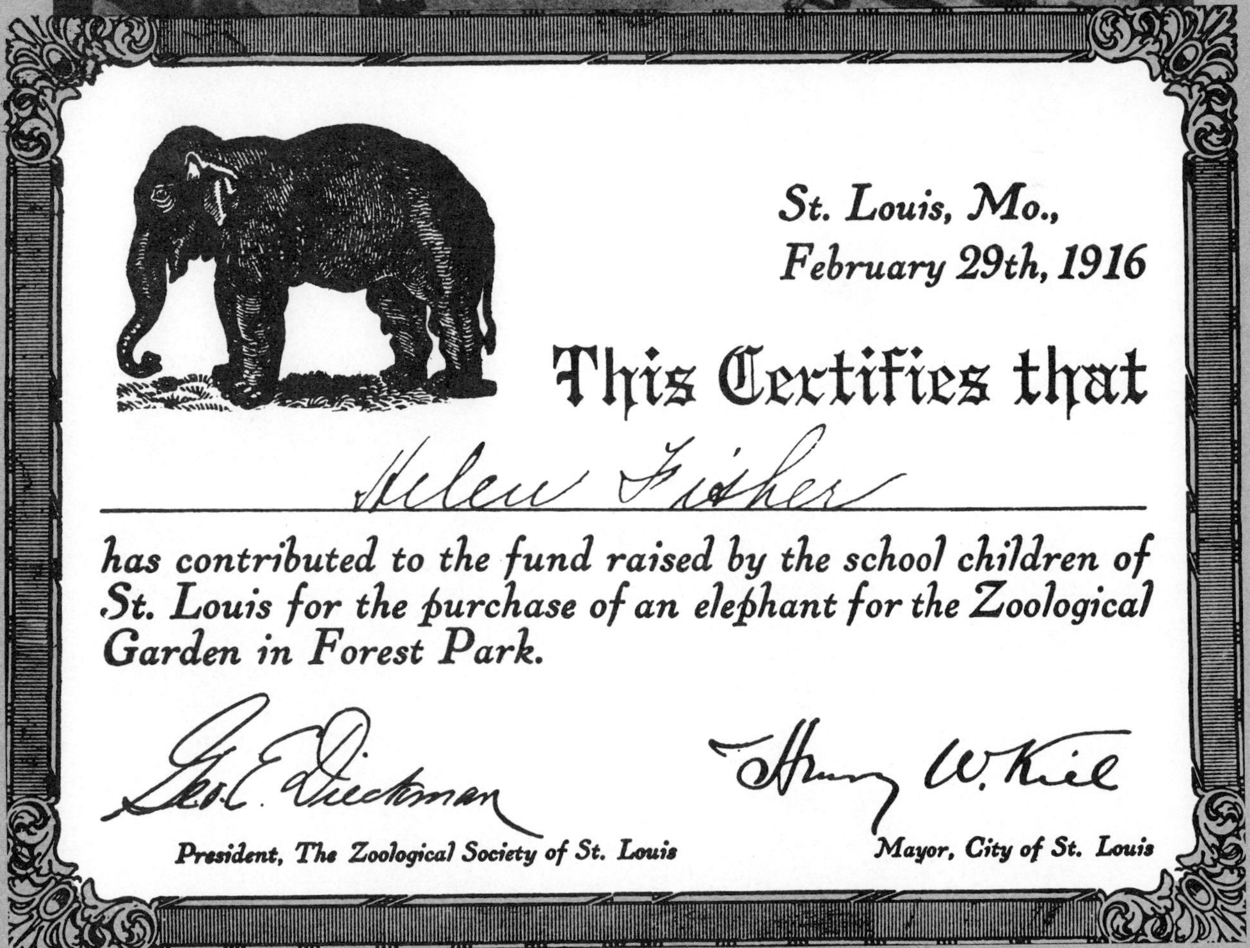

St. Louis, Mo.,
February 29th, 1916

This Certifies that

Helen Fisher

has contributed to the fund raised by the school children of St. Louis for the purchase of an elephant for the Zoological Garden in Forest Park.

Geo. E. Dieckman
President, The Zoological Society of St. Louis

Henry W. Kiel
Mayor, City of St. Louis

around the cage. Without warning, he would splash anyone within range. Phil died in 1958. But thanks to the taxidermist art, he is still on display in the Zoo Association Building. Siegfried, the walrus, and Moby Dick, the sea elephant, also have their share of friends among the visitors to the zoo.

The animals share their fame with a human friend. George P. Vierheller—animal trainer, trader, hero to the city's chimps and children—was zoo director for forty-three years. Vierheller improved the zoo in many ways. He added trained animals shows. A few years ago he set aside an area where children might feed young animals and play with them. A beautiful new Aquatic House was opened in 1961. Here sea animals such as the hippopotamuses, penguins, and seals make their home.

Under the direction of Marlin Perkins, successor to Mr. Vierheller, the St. Louis Zoo Line railroad has been added. Three engines dating from the early steam engine to the modern diesel take turns pulling these cars filled with eager passengers around the zoo area. And so the zoo continues to grow and to delight people from all over the world.

Mr. Vierheller

The Pageant and Masque — Art Hill, 1914

Municipal Opera

In 1914 St. Louis was 150 years old. To celebrate its birthday, St. Louis put on a show in Forest Park on May 28-31. It was given on a large stage built across the lagoon at the foot of Art Hill, and 7500 people took part. The audience sat on the slopes of the hill. The production was entitled "The Pageant and Masque of St. Louis." The pageant told the history of St. Louis. The masque looked into the future of the city.

The success of the show made the leading citizens of St. Louis want to put on another one. For the next two years, annual performances were given in a new place — the spot where our Municipal Opera is today.

A permanent Municipal Theatre was built there in 1917 because the Advertising Club of St. Louis wanted to put on the opera *Aida* for a convention to be held here. The Advertising Club spent $5,000 to start work on the theatre. Concrete aisles and steps were poured immediately. The appearance of famous singers from the Metropolitan and Chicago Opera Companies helped make the performance of *Aida* a great success.

The theatre was used for a patriotic show in July of the next year. But Park Commissioner Nelson Cunliff thought the theatre should be used all summer. He called a meeting of some of the city leaders to talk about it. Two of the men at the meeting were Max Koenigsberg and Arthur Siegel, who had helped plan the *Aida* production. They wanted to use the theatre for light opera. Their enthusiasm was so convincing that they talked the others into it. This committee elected some officers, got a permit to use the theatre, and sent some men to New York to hire showmen.

A decree was granted by the Circuit Court of St. Louis on June 10, 1919, creating the Municipal Theatre Association of St. Louis. That first season opened with a production of *Robin Hood*. Nearly 1400 people came the first night. But it was a rainy night and the show was drowned out. Bridges, stage scenery, costumes, and instruments were washed away. Despite this misfortune the show ran for all scheduled performances, but

133

the attendance was low. Within three weeks the Association was in debt $30,000. Mayor Kiel himself led the fight to keep the opera alive. Nelson Cunliff said that Kiel didn't *ask* people to buy tickets, he *told* them to. Spurred on by the Mayor, men who had already bought more tickets than they would ever use, continued to buy them. The attendance grew and the debt went down. Never again was the Muny Opera in debt.

Every year changes were made to improve the opera. The season was lengthened, a chorus training school was started, and new amplifying equipment was installed. Attendance increased. In 1949 almost 900,000 people went to the opera — the largest attendance the opera has had for a single year. Muny productions have ranged from the classical Gilbert and Sullivan operettas like the *Mikado* to recent Broadway hits like *West Side Story.*

The Opera has brought many well-known stars to St. Louis. Among them are Dorothy Collins, Marion Marlowe, Bob Hope, Penny Singleton, Martyn Green, Hans Conried, Cary Grant, and Irene Dunne. Also, young singers and dancers have started their careers on the muny stage.

In the forty-five years since that shaky start, the Municipal Opera has become the biggest, oldest, and best summer musical theatre in this country.

Jewel Box

T he thick smoke was very hard on plant life in the early 1900's. Both homeowners and the city gardeners wanted to find out what plants would grow best in our smoky city. After a city-wide survey, the newspapers published a list of such plants. The City Park Commissioner asked John Moritz, who was in charge of the city's greenhouses, to display specimens of the plants listed. Moritz's exhibit was such a success that it led to other exhibits in the greenhouses. People flocked to the park — some to learn, others just to admire. Moritz spoke of his display as looking "just like a jewel box," and the name stuck to the greenhouse.

Through the 1920's there was a lot of discussion about having a better setting for flower shows. In 1933, when Bernard Dickmann became mayor, he decided to use available bond issue money to build a new greenhouse.

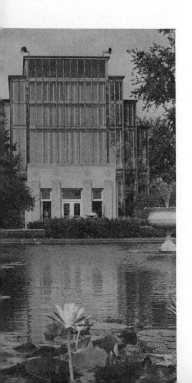

The job fell to William C. E. Becker, the city's chief engineer in charge of buildings and bridges. Becker called on George Pring, who was superintendent of Shaw's Garden, to get some advice on greenhouses.

Becker found that the main threat to greenhouses was from hail-storms, and the greatest damage was always to the top. "It struck me," said Becker, "that the most sensible approach would be to build one that wouldn't get smashed up in the first hailstorm."

This, and not the desire to build something "different," was the reason for the final design of the new Jewel Box. The main roof in the

center and the roofs of each of the setbacks are of metal. It was the first time anyone had built a greenhouse without a glass roof.

This meant that the sunlight would have to come from the sides. Becker and his assistants made more than 2000 readings with light meters at all hours of the day. He then made a model greenhouse and mounted it so that it could be rotated and tilted at any angle. In this way he could measure the amount of light it would receive at any hour of any day. He was convinced that this structure could get plenty of sunlight the year round.

When the city advertised for bids, one of the country's largest builders of greenhouses sent a man to St. Louis. He looked at the plans, said, "It won't work," and didn't even enter a bid. But Becker said it would work, and he was right. The Jewel Box was built. It not only has proved to be a good greenhouse, but it has withstood 27 years of hailstorms, high winds, and even a couple of tornadoes.

The Jewel Box attracts half a million persons every year throughout the United States and abroad by offering nothing more than quiet beauty in a charming and unusual setting.

McDonnell Planetarium

In a beautiful new building on top of the highest hill in Forest Park is one of the country's most interesting planetariums. Inside is a $175,000 projector so delicate and complicated that a team of experts from Japan, where it was made, was needed to put it together. The projector can show what the night sky looked like at some selected time, at almost any time in the past, or what it will probably look like in the future. Movements of the planets and stars can be speeded up. A motion taking the earth 25,800 years to complete is shown in four minutes. All the pictures of the sky are shown by the projector on a dome covered by white perforated aluminum sheets.

The Planetarium visitor may find the experience so pleasurable that he may not realize that he actually learns a great deal. For this reason teachers take entire classes to the Planetarium as a part of their work in science. During a three-year period about twenty-four different programs are given.

The lecture hall seats over four hundred people. On top of the building there is a roof deck for actual night star gazing through large telescopes. The curved upper edge of the building keeps the city's lights from interfering with the views of the stars.

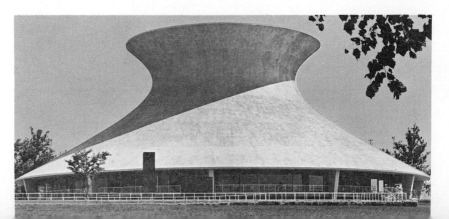

Take Me Out to the Ball Game

On a warm July day in 1860 a game between the "Cyclones" and "Morning Stars" was played at the Old Fairgrounds, but no one bothered to record who won. This was the first organized amateur baseball game played in St. Louis.

By the 1870's there were two professional ball parks in St. Louis. Each was just a piece of ground surrounded by a tight board fence and had a small grandstand. One of these ball parks was on Compton Avenue north of the Pacific Railroad and was owned by the Ranken family. It was called the Red Stocking Park from the color worn by its ball club. The other park, at the Southwest corner of Grand and Sullivan avenues (northern part of Busch Stadium), was owned by the Dunn estate. It was called the St. Louis Ball Park. It was the home of the Browns, so called because they wore brown stockings and brown trim on their uniform. The Empires, Unions, and other amateur clubs played at both of these ball parks.

In 1876 the first league was formed, and a group of St. Louisans sponsored the Browns as one of the member teams. The club lasted only a few years.

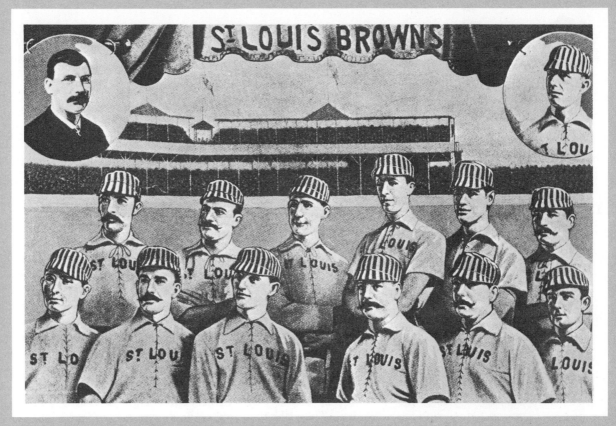

St. Louis Browns—1885. First St. Louis team to win a baseball pennant for St. Louis.

Then Chris Von Der Ahe got into baseball. Chris started out as a clerk in a downtown grocery store and by 1882 owned a grocery and tavern on the corner of Grand and St.  Louis avenues. His store was only a block south of the ball park. Chris noticed that his business had been better when the games at the ball park had been more frequent. So he decided to revive the St. Louis Browns and enter the American Association. "Der Boss President" (as he liked to be called) worked with Al Spink, who suggested that Charley Comiskey be hired as manager and first baseman. Under this leadership the Browns won the World Series of 1886 and the Association pennant from 1885-1888.

In 1892 the National League bought out the American Association, and Von Der Ahe moved his club to another park at Natural Bridge and Vandeventer. But the club started losing ground fast when he sold many stars and tried to direct the club himself. In order to promote the team

he got a loan from a streetcar company and added chute-the-chutes, an all-girl cornet band, a wild west show, big boxing matches, boating, and even night horseracing. But six years later the wooden stands of Von Der Ahe's ball park caught fire during a game and burned to the ground. This was the last straw for Von Der Ahe. He had to sell the park in order to pay the many damage suits. Frank and Stanley Robison, who owned the Cleveland Spiders, became the new owners. They brought most of their Cleveland players with them. The next year the players' stockings and uniform trimmings were changed from brown to red. A sports writer overheard a woman fan say, "What a lovely shade of cardinal." He referred to the team as the "Cardinals" in his column, and it has been known by that name ever since.

In 1901 a new Browns team was entered in the American League. It took over the ball park on Grand Avenue. A violent player war resulted. The Browns' manager raided the Cardinal team for its players. The courts finally had to settle matters and peace was reached between the two major leagues.

Under the ownership of Robert Hedges, the Browns prospered. They tore down their old park to increase the ground space and built Sportsmen's Park — "the finest baseball park in this part of the country" (the present Busch Stadium). That year they finished second, but they did not climb that high again for twenty

years. Two of the outstanding players were first baseman George Sisler, who won batting crowns in 1920 and 1922, and Kenny Williams, who was the home-run king in 1922. The Browns had to go to the final day of the 1944 season before winning a pennant. They lost to the Cardinals in the only All-St. Louis World Series. In its fifty-three year history in St. Louis the Browns won only the one pennant. After the 1953 season the Browns were sold to Baltimore and were renamed the Baltimore Orioles.

Meanwhile, back in the early 1900's the Cardinals struggled along with several big name managers but no pennants. In 1911 Stanley Robison died and his niece Mrs. Helene Robison Britton inherited the club. Lady Bee, as she was known, was quite active as club president, attending all the league meetings in New York. Late in the 1916 season Mrs. Britton sold the sagging Cardinals to a group of stockholders. The price was $375,000, including the ball park and the great Rogers Hornsby, who had recently joined the Cardinal team.

Sam Breadon, who owned a small automobile agency, bought a majority of stock and became the company's first president. A rough period for the Cardinals followed. Breadon had to borrow money from a downtown bank to keep the club in business. But the turning point came when he sold the Vandeventer park to the school board for $200,000 (Beaumont High School stands there today) and rented Sportmen's Park from the Browns, who also continued to use it. Breadon hired Branch

Rickey as field manager and executive vice-president. Rickey was having trouble buying players from the minor clubs. So he bought control of several of the minor league clubs and trained young players on these "farms." This farm system was successful. In 1925 Rogers Hornsby, as manager, brought the team up to fourth place. Then in 1926 came the pennant and World Series victory over the New York Yankees, a team which had such players as Babe Ruth and Lou Gehrig. Between 1926 and 1946 the Cards won the National League pennant nine times and the World Series six times.

The greatest collection of diamond "characters" was the Cardinals' Gashouse Gang of the 1930's. Pepper Martin, Dizzy Dean, Leo Durocher, Frank Frisch, Joe Medwick, Ripper Collins, and Ernie Orsatti were sensations off the diamond as well as on it. The chest slide and the practical joke were among their trademarks. Frisch was manager of this group which winked at many of baseball's stuffy traditions. Once Dizzy and his brother Paul even staged a walk-out strike for more money. But they were brilliant pitchers and in one season accounted for forty-nine victories between them.

St. Louis has had its share of "greats" since the last pennant was won in 1946: Musial (more about him later), Mort and Walker Cooper, Jesse Haines, Urban Shocker, Bill Hallahan, Burleigh Grimes, Howard Pollet, Harry Brecheen, Johnny Mize, Chick Hafey, Terry Moore, Enos Slaughter, Johnny Tobin, Harland Clift, Marty Marion, and Red Schoendienst.

St. Louis was almost without a major league team in 1953. The Browns were sold to Baltimore, and the Cardinals were up for sale. August Busch stepped forward to make sure the Cardinals were not sold to another city. The Redbirds have been in good hands ever since. Busch and St. Louis look forward to many pennants in the new 55,000 seat riverfront stadium.

Civic Center—Busch Memorial Stadium

At 3:47 P.M. on Sunday afternoon, September 29, 1963, Stan—the Man, laid down his bat. This ended twenty-two years with the Cardinals as an active player. He had played more games for one team than any other player in the long history of league baseball.

Stan! the Man!

Life began for Stan in Donora, Pennsylvania, on November 21, 1920. His parents, Mary and Lukacz Musial, were immigrants who worked hard to support their family of six children. Stan, the fifth child — but first son — was his father's pride and joy. As soon as Stan could balance himself at all, his father took him to the Polish National Alliance for weekly workouts in tumbling. Stan loved it. But when he was seven he got his hands on a bat and ball, and all the other games were forgotten.

By the time Stan was ready for Junior High School he was tall, lean, and graceful. One of his gym teachers said, "He had the kind of grace that always seemed to put a boy at the right place at the right time in sports. If he hadn't gone into baseball, he would have been a great basketball player."

But sports weren't the only thing on Stan's mind. He was serious about his studies too. An example of this is the story told about Stan when he took algebra. It seems that he got through the first three years of high school without it. It wasn't required for graduation, but Stan thought he should take it anyway. In order to do that he had to go back to the junior high school. Naturally the other students were much younger and smaller than 17-year-old, 6-foot tall Stan. Most boys wouldn't risk the ridicule of their friends by doing such a thing—but it did not stop Stan. One of his friends said, "Here was the measure of a champion. He dared to be different."

One of the things that Stan's father wanted most for his son was a college education. But if baseball was his son's choice, then he would not stand in the way. Stan's father gave his approval and signed a contract for his under-age son to play ball for five months at $65 a month.

After his second season with a Class D team at Williamson, West Virginia, Stan went home to Donora and married Lillian Labash. The wedding was November 21 — Stan's nineteenth birthday. He took his young bride with him the next season. He was still in Class D but went to Daytona Beach this time. The manager of this club was Dick Kerr, a former major leaguer. Kerr worked very well with the young players and took a personal interest in each one.

Stan, a left hander, was mainly a pitcher during those early years, but because there were so few men on the teams, they often had to play another position as well. One August day when he was playing center field, he caught a low line drive but fell heavily on his left shoulder. The shoulder was badly bruised. He was able to pitch twice after that, but he knew that he would not be able to pitch any more. Stan was afraid that he was finished as a ball player at the age of nineteen. He took his troubles to Dick Kerr. Kerr not only talked Stan out of quitting — he helped him out financially by renting a large home and inviting Stan and Lil to live with him and his wife. The Musials remained grateful to the Kerrs. In fact, when their first child was born they named him for Dick.

With Kerr's help and encouragement Stan played well enough that season to be promoted to Class AA at Columbus, Ohio. This was just one step under the major leagues. Branch Rickey of the Cards kept his eye on the young players at Columbus. The manager of the team was Burt Shotton, who had a reputation as a hard man to please. Deciding to keep his troubles to himself, Stan didn't tell Shotton about his bad arm. He worked out regularly with the pitchers. Shotton noticed that he couldn't throw too well, but he also noticed that he was a good batter. One day when Rickey came to see the players, Stan was playing in the outfield. Rickey said, "That man's not a pitcher; he's an outfielder." But even an outfielder had to throw, and Stan couldn't. His arm was too sore for anything but a lob. But time and exercise helped his arm, and soon he was throwing satisfactorily. His arm was no longer dead, and he knew he could hit. Then Stan got the call to join the Cardinals.

The Cards were playing a double-header against the Boston Braves. During the first game, young Musial (not yet twenty-one) sat on the bench. In the second game Manager Billy Southworth decided to rest Terry Moore, who had been hurt in an earlier game. He moved rightfielder Johnny Hopp to Moore's position in center and put Musial in rightfield. Old Jim Tobin, pitching for Boston, was famous for his knuckleball. His first time at bat in the major leagues, Stan watched the pitch wander toward the plate. He wound up and swung so hard he fell down after he missed it. He had never seen a knuckler before. On the second pitch he tied himself in a knot trying to hit the ball — but managed to hit a pop fly that time. Two innings later Musial faced Tobin again. There were two men on base. Tobin threw Stan another knuckler, but Stan was ready for that one. He waited until the ball reached home plate and then hit it against the concrete wall in right center field for a double. Both runners scored and the Cards won the game, 3-2. Great days for Stan had begun.

Everyone wanted to see young Musial during the next spring training. Stan knew he was causing a stir, and he really tried to play well. But his shoulder was acting up, and he just couldn't hit. Sports writers went away from spring training shaking their heads.

But Southworth had faith in Musial and opened the season with him in left field. Stan got off to a bad start. He couldn't throw, and he couldn't hit. Southworth had to bench him. He let Stan sit in the dugout and watch. This gave Stan a chance to relax and regain his confidence. After a while Southworth put him back in the game against righthanded pitchers. Stan really slashed the ball then. The Cards went on to win the pennant and the World Series with rookie Musial batting .315.

One of the problems that year was Stan's habit of falling down. He took tumbles while chasing fly balls. When he continued to do this the next year, Dr. Weaver, the Card trainer, decided to look into the matter. He found that Stan had bought a new pair of shoes when he joined the club. The shoes were too small for Stan, but being a thrifty fellow, he didn't want to throw them away. So he played in the tight shoes and fell down because his balance wasn't as good as it should have been. When Weaver discovered the cause, he put Stan in a cab, drove to the nearest sporting goods store, and bought him a pair of shoes that fit. Stan stopped falling down.

Stan's throwing arm continued to improve, and by the time he went into the Navy in 1945 he was a good batter and a sound outfielder. When he returned from the Navy in 1946, he assumed that he would continue in the outfield. But the Cards traded their best first baseman, and halfway through the season they needed someone new on first base. Stan could handle ground balls well and had good body control, so he was asked to take over.

During this same season, the Mexican League was raiding the majors for ballplayers by offering them fantastic salaries. Stan was making just under $15,000. He was offered $100,000 to break his contract with the Cards. Other major leaguers had accepted the offers, but Stan knew that he could never face his son Dick if he did anything like that. He flatly refused the offer.

In May of 1948 the Cardinals played the Dodgers in a three-game series at Ebbets Field. During that series, Stan made nine hits in fifteen time at bat. It seemed to the Dodger fans that every time they looked up Musial was headed plateward. The fans moaned, "Here comes that man again." And that's where the name "the Man" was born. Now millions of Americans call him "the Man," and they mean it in every sense of the word.

Stan's fans

Stan is not just a ballplayer with more than fifty major league records and a roomful of trophies and plaques — he is a blend of talent, unselfishness, dignity, and humility. The stories of Musial's quiet kindnesses are endless. There was the time when a Santa Claus, headed for an orphan home, was sidetracked and Stan dropped his own decorating on Christmas Eve to take his place. In 1958, after he got his 3,000th major league base hit, he quietly bought a home for the retired Kerrs in Houston as a token of his appreciation for their help in his early years. He wanted no one to know about it except his wife and the Kerrs, but a reporter heard about it, and the story was too good to be kept quiet.

Stan is a good family man too. Lillian says, "He is strict with the children, and if their school work isn't up to what it should be, there are serious sessions." When Dick graduated from college, Stan asked his first favor of the Cardinals — to be excused to attend the ceremonies.

On a windy Sunday afternoon in September, 1963, 27,576 fans turned out to pay their respects to Stan, the Man. There was an hourlong tribute before Stan's final game. He received gifts ranging from a Boy Scout neckerchief to a ring from his teammates with the familiar Number 6 set in diamonds. Civic, political, and baseball leaders honored him with heartwarming messages. Two planes flew over Busch Stadium bearing the message, "We salute the Man."

During the game that followed Stan made two hits as he had in his first game twenty-two years earlier. This brought his total hits to 3630 in 3025 games.

As Stan hung up his No. 6 uniform (the number has not been used since), he became a vice president for the Cardinal Club. Later he was made director of the nation's Physical Fitness Program. . . . But baseball isn't the same without Stan, the Man.

ARTS

WITH A SONG IN OUR HEARTS

St. Louis has always been a musical city. In the founding days dancing was a popular activity, and the merry fiddlers played for the French quadrilles and cotillions. In the early 1800's the Cathedral had a choir and gave special attention to vocal music. An Italian named Merilano came by invitation of Bishop Rosati to introduce the organ. The large German influx in the 1840's and 1850's was responsible for arousing interest in several kinds of music. Musical societies, gesangvereins (singing societies), and brass bands were organized. Musicians from other nationalties —

Eleazar de Carvalho, Conductor St. Louis Symphony Orchestra

Irish, Spanish, Italian, and Polish — all did their part in making music a part of the life of the city. In the 1890's St. Louis became important in the development of ragtime and jazz, and during the last half century the most notable feature of the city's musical history has become the emergence of singers who found their way to the Metropolitan Opera in New York.

The St. Louis Symphony Orchestra, second oldest in the country, was the result of popular interest in choral music. The singing societies are not as prominent now as then, but the traditions continue in organizations such as the Liederkranz Society and the Bach Choir. The St. Louis Choral Society was created in 1880. A few years later, the name was changed to the St. Louis Choral-Symphony Society. Joseph Otten became the first conductor of the St. Louis Symphony Orchestra, which was an outgrowth of the earlier society. He was followed

by Alfred Ernst, Max Zach, Rudolph Ganz, Vladimir Golschmann, Edouard Van Remoortel, and Eleazar de Carvalho, the present conductor. For some years the St. Louis Symphony Orchestra has provided special concerts for school children. The St. Louis Philharmonic Society was founded in 1860, twenty years before the Symphony. Members of generations of St. Louis families have played in what has been called the finest non-professional orchestra in the United States. Even now only the conductor and soloists are professional, but every player must pass an annual audition.

Ragtime music became a favorite with St. Louisans near the end of the nineteenth century when the riverboats still made their swing between New Orleans and St. Louis. Every waterfront saloon had a lively piano player in those days when the levee was bustling with activity. Negro pianists with a syncopated, choppy style combined the heritage of spirituals and plantation melodies, work songs, military marches, and country dances to produce the forerunner of what we now call jazz. Scott Joplin was one of the popular ragtime artists; his "Maple Leaf Rag" is probably the best known of the "rags." Tom Turpin not only ran the Rosebud Cafe on Market Street but wrote down the difficult notation and had the music published. His "rags" in sheet music form were made available in America in the five-and-ten-cent stores. Even today the Dixieland jazz played in Gaslight Square by Singleton Palmer's group harkens back to that era.

Paul Tietjens was a native St. Louisan who composed songs, piano pieces, chamber works, and sonatas. Through a lucky accident, while studying and writing in Chicago, he met Frank Baum, who had written the book *Wizard of Oz*. Baum was looking for someone to help him make a musical comedy out of the book. Twenty-five year old Tietjens proved to be the man. The *Wizard of Oz* was such a success that it had a five-year run in Chicago, was made into a movie, and has been seen on our Muny Opera stage. Tietjens later became musical director for Maude Adams, famous

actress, but most of the remainder of his life he spent in Europe studying and writing.

St. Louis has given stars to the Metropolitan Opera since the Roaring Twenties, when Marian Telva and Elda Vettori were hailed as successes in New York. Helen Traubel, of more recent opera fame, often calls herself "The St. Louis Woman." She was born at Jefferson and Chouteau avenues above her father's drugstore. A graduate of Wyman School, she loved to sing but was not in a hurry for a musical career. It was not until Walter Damrosch visited St. Louis to conduct the Sangerfest (singing society convention) and heard her that she began to consider a career in music away from St. Louis. He was so elated over her voice that he offered her a chance to sing in his opera *The Man Without a Country* soon to open in New York. The opera lasted only five performances, but the National Broadcasting Company offered her a $10,000 contract. She tore it up because the music she was to sing was not to her liking. She returned home, accepting work as soloist at the Pilgrim Congregational Church and at the United Hebrew Temple. Mme. Vetta Karst, under whom she studied for seventeen

Paul Tietjens   Characters in the Wizard of Oz

Helen Traubel

contestant in the 1953 Metropolitan Opera auditions and was named the winner unanimously. After more study he made a stirring debut in the Met production of *Aida.* He is presently giving concerts, and he has opened a music school in Los Angeles.

Another opera personality is the beauteous Jean Browning Madeira. Reared in St. Louis and taught piano by her musically trained mother, Jean started out as a pianist. She was so good that she was awarded a scholarship to the Julliard School of Music. She happened to sing for her teacher one day and was advised to study voice rather than piano. After gaining experience with the Chautauqua Opera Company, she went to the Met and became a favorite. She is especially well-known for her interpretation of the title role of *Carmen.*

The latest St. Louisan who has become a national and international star on the musical horizon is Grace Bumbry. Grace, still in her twenties, is another musical great who started with the study of the piano. Her parents and two brothers, however, all sang in the choir at the Union Memorial Methodist Church. She learned all the songs by tagging along to rehearsals with them. It wasn't until she reached Sumner High School and came to the attention of the director of vocal music, Kenneth Billups, that she received training.

Several important things happened to Grace in her seventeenth year. She sang and won first prize at the National Association of Negro Musicians and took top honors on the Teen O'Clock Time program sponsored by Station KMOX. Curt Ray, disc jockey on that program, became interested in her and helped her receive an audition with Arthur Godfrey. Mr. Godfrey was greatly impressed by her performance.

Miss Bumbry, through the assistance of scholarships and donations, studied at Boston and Northwestern Universities. She later enrolled at the Music Academy of the West to study with Mme. Lotte Lehmann and received a hearing by famous contralto Marian Anderson, Grace Bumbry's idol. After winning the John Hay Whitney Fund Fellowship, Miss Bumbry took off for Europe, where she studied for a year with the Vienna State Opera Company. She scored a hit at the Wagnerian Festival in Bayreuth, Germany. Shortly afterward she signed a five year contract with Sol Hurok,

years, was very stern, and Miss Traubel remarked one day, "I can never satisfy you." Mme. Karst snapped back, "When you can satisfy me you won't need me anymore." Miss Traubel returned to New York and prepared for a debut in Town Hall. By this time she was thirty-six years old, pounds heavier, but with a voice so improved that in a short time she was singing Wagnerian roles. Helen Traubel has been a Metropolitan Opera star (and St. Louis baseball fan) for years, but she has not limited herself to opera. She surprised the music world when she turned to Broadway and night club singing.

Robert McFerrin, a graduate of Sumner High School, was the second Negro to sing at the Metropolitan Opera. (Marian Anderson, noted contralto, was the first.) He had no idea, in his high school days, that he would ever be a singer. His teacher, Wirt Walton, did though and told him he had a voice that would someday make the Met. McFerrin studied at Fisk University and the Chicago College of Music until he was drafted into the army. When he got out of the army he did solo work at Temple Israel. It was through the financial aid of Mrs. David Kriegshaber, Temple Israel organist, that he got to New York for further study. There he caught the eye of Boris Goldovsky, who offered him a scholarship role in the opera department of Tanglewood in Massachusetts. He became a

*Grace Brumby—
international
opera star*

Command performance for the Kennedys at the White House

renowned impresario. Her fame was further enhanced by a White House Command Performance at the invitation of the late President and Mrs. John F. Kennedy.

St. Louis is a musical city. We enjoy performances of the Civic Opera and Little Symphony Concerts at Washington University as well as jazz concerts at Kiel Auditorium. There are singing groups such as the Cosmopolitan Singers and also gospel choirs and rock and roll groups that bring pleasure to many. We listen proudly to new stars like Carolee Combs and Eugene Holmes and composer-arranger Oliver Nelson. Whatever your musical taste, you may be sure it can be satisfied in St. Louis.

W. C. Handy

The SAINT LOUIS BLUES
has been sung, danced, played, whistled and
chanted in every nook and cranny of
the globe. If you mention St. Louis in Iowa
or Indonesia, some people will think first
of the song that has immortalized our city.

Saint
Louis
Blues

It was late in the 1800's when William Christopher Handy arrived in St. Louis with a quartette he had organized in Birmingham, Alabama. They had heard that musicians prospered here. This was not entirely true. Handy's group found that it was very hard to get work, and they finally had to disband.

Nineteen-year old William Handy found part-time jobs, but they didn't last long. Many nights Handy spent sleeping on the cobblestones of the levee. When he could get a dime for his day's meal, he bought a loaf of bread and some butter and molasses to dip it in.

It was on one of those "down days" that he stood outside the door of a saloon listening to a guitar-playing singer doing a chorus of *Afterwards*. The second verse, "Sometimes my heart grows weary of its sadness, sometimes my heart grows weary of its pain," struck him. Handy was weary too, but the music made him forget his dirty, tattered clothes and drew him in. The bartender was about to throw him out when he found that Handy could play the guitar and sing. He played tune after tune. The crowd got up a collection for him, and he was invited to come and sing again.

The many sights and sounds heard on the river were rooted in Handy's mind for the rest of his life. He recalled in his memoirs: "I don't think I'd want to forget the high-roller Stetson hats of the men and the diamonds the girls wore in their ears." Along the levee he heard the chants of work songs, levee blues, and the shouts of the roustabouts dancing a trot to the plinking of banjos.

Fourteen years later, in Memphis one night, Handy put together many of these sights and sounds in *The Saint Louis Blues*. The misery he had suffered bore fruit in song and changed his life. He had written other music, but it had not made much money. This time he contacted a publishing company that agreed to print 10,000 copies. The song soon became a hit, and Handy found both musical and financial success. He opened his own publishing house and became a member of the American Society of Composers and Publishers.

Mr. Handy died in 1958, but he will be remembered in St. Louis by Handy Park, Euclid and Ashland, and the memorial to him to be built on the riverfront.

Louis Armstrong plays Saint Louis Blues *at a benefit for the St. Louis Symphony, on the steamer* Admiral, *in 1963*

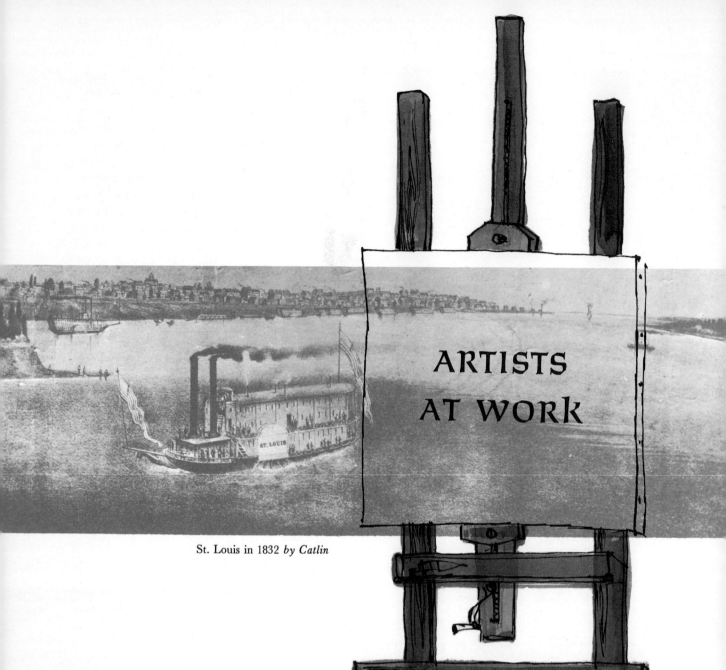

St. Louis in 1832 *by Catlin*

ARTISTS AT WORK

The Mississippi and Missouri rivers played an important part in the history of art in St. Louis. Some of the earliest artists who painted here were inspired by the scenery of the rivers, the Indians who lived on the banks, or the boatmen who poled their way through the waters.

Philadelphia artist George Catlin was one of those who wanted to paint the Indians along the rivers. Coming to St. Louis in 1830, he was granted permission to enter Indian country by General William Clark, Superintendent of Indian Affairs, whose home and office were in this city. Catlin went on trips up the Missouri

and Mississippi, painting scenes of Indian life; but he did some of his work here in St. Louis.

Catlin and Clark became good friends. With his stool and easel at the General's side, Catlin sketched Indian visitors who came to Clark's council hall. At Jefferson Barracks Catlin also found Indians to draw. After an Indian war, Chief Black Hawk and other defeated Indians were brought to the Barracks as prisoners. Heavy balls and chains were fastened to their ankles, but they posed for Catlin willingly.

During his stay in St. Louis, Catlin painted *St. Louis in 1832*. This picture shows a steamboat on the Mississippi River with the city in

Street in St. Louis *by Lewis*

the background. You can see it at the Missouri Historical Society. Catlin's painting and one by St. Louisan Leon Pomarede, *A View of St. Louis—1832*, are the earliest paintings of the city.

Henry Lewis, another artist who lived in St. Louis for some time, also painted views of the city. His *St. Louis in 1846* and *Street in St. Louis* are in the City Art Museum. Lewis is remembered especially for his pictures of rivers. He made a panorama of Mississippi River scenes almost 4000 feet long and twelve feet high. Wound on cylinders, it took two hours to unroll. St. Louisans of 1849 could view the "moving picture" for fifty cents. St. Louis became a production center for this popular kind of entertainment. Pomarede also painted a panorama. When he traveled up the Mississippi River to get material for it, he took along an apprentice artist — Carl Wimar.

Like Catlin, Carl Wimar wanted to paint Indians. Having arrived here from Germany at the age of fifteen, he had moved with his family into a house near a favorite camping ground of the Indians — the block between Thirteenth and Fourteenth streets near Olive, where the Public Library now stands. Indians stayed on those grounds when they came to St. Louis to sell their furs to the American Fur Company, which had its headquarters here.

Carl was a shy boy, but he made friends easily with his red-skinned neighbors. Tramping the woods with them, he learned to understand them. On his trip up the Mississippi River with his teacher, he had another good chance to study Indians. Then, scraping together a small sum of money, he went to Düsseldorf, Germany, to study. Four years later, in 1857,

he was back in St. Louis, ready to paint the story of the American Indian.

Wimar found that St. Louis no longer had its Indian visitors. The American Fur Company had set up posts along the Missouri River, and the Indians took their furs there instead of bringing them to St. Louis. Wimar made several trips up the Missouri River, on American Fur Company steamboats, to make sketches for his paintings. On one of these trips, besides his painting equipment, he took a camera. Most of his photographs had to be taken from quite a distance, however. The frightened Indians usually fled as soon as the strange-looking box was set up.

After his return to St. Louis, Wimar made many paintings of the Indians and buffalo he had seen on his trip. They were good pictures, but they did not become popular immediately. Like many painters of the day, he was forced to paint portraits to earn a living.

By and by, however, Wimar's work attracted attention. In 1862 Wimar was chosen for the important task of decorating the inside of the dome of the Old Courthouse. But for some time he had had tuberculosis, and as he worked on the murals his health grew steadily worse.

Chief Billy Bowlegs *by Wimar*

Raftsmen Playing Cards *by Bingham*

He had to be carried up the long flights of steps to his scaffold, where a couch was placed so that he could rest frequently. While he was painting the last panel, he died. The murals soon faded and peeled, but a few years ago some of them were restored. You can see them today if you visit the Old Courthouse. At the Art Museum you will find some of his other paintings of Indian life, including *Buffalo Dance* and *Chief Billy Bowlegs*. His picture of a St. Louis brewery of that day is there too. You can see *Hunting the Buffalo* and several of his portraits of St. Louisans at the Missouri Historical Society.

The greatest of the river artists, George Caleb Bingham, spent a year in St. Louis painting portraits. In the 1840's he had an exhibition here of some of the pictures of Missouri flatboatmen that made him famous. Many of his paintings can be seen today in the Mercantile Library, the City Art Museum, the Missouri Historical Society, and the Boatmen's Bank Building. Bingham made careful drawings of the people he intended to put in his paintings. Over a hundred of these drawings have been preserved in a *Sketch Book* at the Mercantile Library.

Later artists of St. Louis found many different subjects for their paintings, but Indians remained a favorite with some of them. One such artist was Oscar Berninghaus. Like many young men who wanted to become artists in the 1880's, he worked as a lithographer's apprentice. Then, as a commercial artist, he made designs for posters for the Anheuser-Busch brewery. His strong, bold pictures of the brewery's famous Clydesdale horses and of events in the city's history became well-known in St. Louis. For many years he also designed floats for the Veiled Prophet parade.

When he was about twenty-five years old, Berninghaus made a trip to the little Pueblo town of Taos and immediately became interested in its Indians and their horses. From then on Taos was where he wanted to live. When he was about fifty, he was finally able to make his home there. He became a highly respected artist, known for his paintings of Indians. One of them, *Peace and Plenty*, shows an elderly Indian brave and an Indian woman looking with pleased faces at the corn, squashes, and pumpkins spread out before them.

Indians and the West attracted another noted St. Louis artist, Charles Russell, who was born here in 1865. Russell's family was well-known in the city. His grandfather owned a big piece of land of which the present Russell Boulevard was a part.

As a boy, Charles sketched on margins of his school books, on his tablets, and even on sidewalks and front steps. When he was twelve years old, one of his drawings took first prize at the St. Louis County Fair. But Charles was not interested in school. Often he played hooky to hang around the riverfront. When he was in his teens, his parents let him go to Montana

Still Life *by Quest*

with a family friend for a visit to the friend's sheep ranch. They hoped he would settle down when he returned and go into their clay tile business. But Charles stayed in Montana for the rest of his life — forty-six years.

In Montana, Russell became a cowboy, a painter, and a sculptor. He loved the open range, its Indians, and its animal life. Everyone liked him for his story-telling and his humor. Known as the "cowboy painter," he lived a carefree, untidy life, often wearing a shirt until it could almost stand up by itself. Later he married and settled down. By the time of his death in 1925, Russell had become famous. In the City Art Museum you can see some of his sculpture of the Indians and animals of the West.

Indians and Scouts Talking *by Russell*

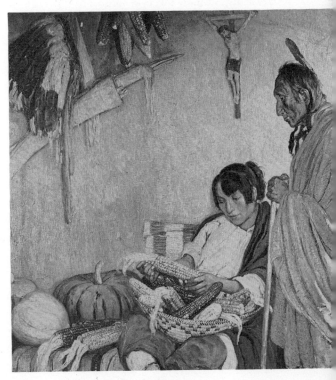

Peace and Plenty *by Berninghaus*

155

Present-day St. Louis has many famous artists. One of the best known is Charles Quest. For many years he has been a full-time painter, sculptor, and print maker. Since 1945 Quest has taught drawing at Washington University. His pictures are in museums throughout the world. Several years ago when the Old Cathedral was being restored, Quest was chosen to paint a copy of a famous picture for the space above its altar. To make this eight-by-fourteen-foot copy, Quest had a wall torn out and a new studio built in the rear of his home in Creve Coeur. There, using photographs, he did the early work on his painting. Then he flew to Madrid to make a firsthand study of the original painting, which hangs in a museum there. Later that year he completed the picture.

St. Louisan Fred Conway, born in 1900, has won many art awards. He was one of five American artists chosen to paint a decoration for the United Nations Building in 1955. His art training included classes at Washington University, study in Paris, and travel in North America.

Fred Conway

You can see paintings by Conway in the lobby of Barnes Hospital. Murals he painted are in the offices of Peabody Coal Company on Third Street and in the Brown Shoe Company building in Clayton. Conway feels that painting murals sweeps him into the life of the people around him, and he puts many of those people into his murals. Because high places "scare him to death," however, it takes him a month to work up the courage to start one of them. His favorite corner, Grand and Olive, turns up in many of his pictures. A painting of his, *Green Bird*, hangs in the Art Museum.

St. Louis artist Martyl Schweig Langsdorf is a former pupil of Hamilton School. Martyl chose to use only her first name because her mother, Aimee Schweig, was an established artist, and Martyl wanted her work to be judged for itself alone. Her father, Martin Schweig, was a well-known St. Louis photographer.

Martyl attended Mary Institute and Washington University. She spent the summers at Ste. Genevieve, where her mother conducted an art school. Always interested in people and the way they lived, Martyl used to spend a great deal of time in downtown St. Louis,

Landscape by Martyl

making notes and sketches. Then she would go home and paint what she had seen.

Martyl has won many prizes for her art work. At the City Art Museum you can see several of her paintings.

Siegfried Reinhardt is another noted St. Louis painter. Born in Germany, he was brought to America by his parents at the age of three. From his early childhood he was eager to draw. Sometimes, as a boy, he spent half the night copying the work of famous German artists.

Reinhardt went to St. Louis public schools. At thirteen, he attended a special course, taught by Charles Quest, for gifted high school students. Except for this course, he taught himself almost everything he knows in art. When he went to Washington University after service in the army, he was advised to take his degree in another subject because he already knew so much about art. He is an art instructor at Washington University.

Among his many honors, Reinhardt was chosen by the National Park Service Board to do a mural on the Westward Movement for the museum beneath the Gateway Arch on the Riverfront. You can see his painting, *Pieta*, which won first prize at an art show, in the City Art Museum.

In the museums and art galleries of St. Louis is exhibited the work of other St. Louisans. Many excellent sculptures are in the city's public places. Nancy Coonsman Hahn's fountain in Lucas Garden behind the Central Public Library, Walker Hancock's *Zuni Indian Bird Charmer* near the Bird Cage in Forest Park, Harriet Hosmer's statue of Senator Benton in Lafayette Park are only a few of them.

Siegfried Reinhardt

Eugene Field

Eugene Field House

Poetry, Prose, and Prizes

Of the authors who have helped make our city famous, one of the best known to St. Louisans is Eugene Field. Born in St. Louis in 1850, Field spent his early years in a house at 634 South Broadway. When he was six years old his mother died, and he went to live with an aunt in Massachusetts. Later he worked for newspapers in St. Louis and other cities. In Chicago he wrote a popular daily column called "Sharps and Flats."

All through his life Eugene Field had a great love for children. On the way to his own wedding he stopped to settle a quarrel between two boys on the street. A messenger found the missing bridegroom down on his knees in the dirt playing marbles. Because of his poems for young people Field is called "the children's poet." You have probably read some of these poems. One of the best known is "Little Boy Blue."

The Field home on South Broadway, which is owned by the St. Louis Board of Education, was restored some years ago with the help of pennies and nickels from the children of the St. Louis public schools. Field's family sent many of their old possessions for the restored house. Other personal belongings were brought here from Field's Chicago home, where he died in 1895.

Today, on the first two floors of the Field house you can see reminders of the poet. The stiff linen cuffs with the cuff links still in them, the silk skull cap he wore at night, his heelless slippers, and a blue and white striped necktie are all on display. Several manuscripts in Field's small neat handwriting can be seen in the exhibit cases. Each year a Christmas tree is put up and decorated in the way it was done when Field was living.

Brandt Home

Another well-known St. Louis writer had the same name as a famous British statesman — Winston Churchill. He was born in 1871 at 2641 Olive Street, lived for a time at 2810 Pine Street, and attended Smith Academy. He left St. Louis to enroll in the United States Naval Academy at Annapolis and did not return until after he had resigned from the Navy and had become a writer.

Churchill came back to St. Louis to write *The Crisis*, a story of Civil War times in St. Louis. He spent days in the Mercantile Library, looking through newspaper files and reading about places and characters that were to play a part in his book. One of the settings of the story is "Bellegarde," a beautiful home on the bluffs overlooking the Mississippi, just west of Broadway between Grand and Bissell. Many noted people were entertained in this home, among them General Ulysses S. Grant and General William T. Sherman. James E. Yeatman was married there. Yeatman was one of the men who organized the Western Sanitary Commission to take care of the sick and wounded during the Civil War. Grant, Sherman, and Yeatman — under the name of Mr. Brinsmade — are all characters in Churchill's book.

Churchill used the Brandt home on Eighth and Chouteau as the scene of another part of his story. This house was rented by General John C. Fremont, a Union Civil War officer, for his headquarters. Here he issued a proclamation freeing the slaves sixteen months before President Lincoln's Emancipation Proclamation went into effect. In Churchill's book *The Crisis*, the heroine, dressed in the Confederate colors, red and white, stands defiantly in front of the house as General Fremont mounts his horse. The Brandt home was torn down in 1902, but the old horse-mounting block is still there.

"Bellegarde"

Through William Marion Reedy, St. Louis literature really got its start. Reedy grew up, with many other Irish Americans, near Sixth and Carr streets in a part of our city that is known as Kerry Patch. After his graduation from high school, he was a newspaper reporter for several years.

In 1891 he became editor of a weekly magazine called the *Sunday Mirror* and later the *Mirror*. Before long the *Mirror* was read all over the country. Reedy wrote excellent essays for his magazine. It was said that he could make even a broomstick sound interesting. His reviews of books by important authors helped St. Louisans know and like good literature. When Reedy praised a book, people rushed to read it.

Reedy published the work of many gifted writers who were not yet known. Because of his encouragement Edgar Lee Masters, an Illinois poet, wrote the book that made him famous — *Spoon River Anthology*. Many young authors in our city began their literary careers by writing for the *Mirror*.

William Marion Reedy

Sara Teasdale

Outstanding among these young St. Louisans was Sara Teasdale. Miss Teasdale had gone to Mary Institute, a private school which was then at Lake and Waterman avenues. Later she studied at Washington University. After spending a year in Europe with her mother, she and her family moved from their home in the 3600 block of Lindell Boulevard to a luxurious home near Forest Park in fashionable Kingsbury Place. Sara Teasdale was a quiet, thoughtful person who had been brought up to think she was sickly. She often stayed in her room for days at a time to save her strength. But she also spent many hours writing simple but beautiful poems. You have probably read the one called "Stars." A book of hers, *Love Songs*, won a poetry prize given by Columbia University.

Reedy also published the work of Zoë Akins, the daughter of a wealthy politician who had

Fanny Hurst

160

once been the St. Louis postmaster. This lively young woman found time to ride horseback, hunt, fish, and paint pictures, besides writing poetry and reviews for the *Mirror*. In 1935 her play, *The Old Maid*, won the Pulitzer Prize.

Fannie Hurst is another St. Louis writer whom Reedy helped. Even as a girl at Central High School, Fannie wanted to become a writer. In her comfortable home at 5641 Cates Avenue she pounded out story after story on her typewriter. In 1909, when she was a student at Washington University, her English teacher praised one of her themes highly. Miss Hurst slipped it into an envelope, took it down to Reedy's office, and dropped it through a slot in the door. Several weeks later she found it printed in the *Mirror*. Her life as a writer had begun. Moving to New York, Fannie Hurst worked as a salesgirl, an actress, a nursemaid, and a factory worker. These experiences helped her write about real life. Fannie Hurst is the author of many books. A recent one, *Anatomy of Me,* tells the story of her life.

Like Fannie Hurst, Shirley Seifert was graduated from Central High School and Washington University. She is one of several modern St. Louis authors who have written books about their city. Four of her many novels have St. Louis backgrounds, and she recently wrote *Key to St. Louis,* part of a national series of guidebooks. Her historical novels are based on careful research and much note-taking. When Miss Seifert's first story was published in 1919 she decided to stay in St. Louis, her favorite city, and her home is still in this area.

A world-famous writer born in St. Louis is Thomas S. Eliot, winner of a Nobel Prize for Literature. From the time of his birth in 1888 until he was sixteen years old, he lived at 2635 Locust Street in St. Louis. His grandfather was Reverend William Greenleaf Eliot, the founder of Washington University. Though T. S. Eliot moved to England and wrote his books and plays there, in some ways he remained a St. Louisan. The Eads Bridge over the Mississippi River, the steamboats on the levee, the ragged coats of buffalo he saw in Forest Park, a fog that hung over the city, all stayed in his memory. The name Prufrock in one of his writings is a name he saw on a sign over a shop in this city. T. S. Eliot's mother, father, and grandfather are buried in Bellefontaine Cemetery.

Among recent writers having some connection with St. Louis the most renowned is playwright Tennessee Williams. His family moved to St. Louis from Mississippi in 1918 when he was a boy of seven. Many of his memories of St. Louis are not happy ones. The children at school made fun of his southern accent. His home life was unhappy too; he felt that his father treated him harshly. Although Williams left St. Louis while still a young man, he began his life as a writer in this city, and *The Glass Menagerie,* the play which established him as a playwright, has a St. Louis setting. Since the opening of that production in 1945, Williams has won the Pulitzer Prize for two other dramas — *A Streetcar Named Desire* and *A Cat on a Hot Tin Roof.*

Shirley Seifert

T. S. Eliot

Libraries

Many early St. Louisans were well educated men who owned their own libraries. Most of these were kept in the homes of the owners — but not all. It is recorded that a Mr. Beverly Tucker had his library and study in the trunk of a hollow tree.

Libraries as most St. Louisans know them began in 1824 when a semipublic library was started. A fee of $5 was charged, payable in either books or money. At the year's end there were 1,106 books and 181 shares in money.

The Mercantile Library was established in 1846. It was the first large library west of the Mississippi and was housed in a large brick building on Fifth and Locust. The first floor of the building was rented to shopkeepers, the second floor was completely occupied by the library, and the third was used for a public hall. At the end of the first year there were 1,680 books in the library. Today, it has on its shelves about 170,000 books.

Visitors can see a number of interesting items there. One is the first fourteen pages of Chouteau's original journal describing the founding and settling of St. Louis. Another is a copy of the third issue of the *Missouri Gazette,* first paper west of the Mississippi. Early maps, restaurant menus, theater programs, and a genuine $3 bill issued by the Bank of Missouri in 1818 and bearing the signature of Auguste Chouteau, the bank's president, are other items in the old library's rich collection.

In 1860 the Public Library was started by Ira Divoll, superintendent of schools, in connection with the public schools. It was on Olive and Fifth. During the first year the Board of Education spent $5000 and bought 1500 books.

Frederick M. Crunden was librarian from 1877 to 1909. Through his hard work a library tax was passed in 1893, and thereafter the library was free to the public.

The St. Louis Public Library is now located in a beautiful building at Thirteenth and Olive. The cost of that building, which was opened in 1912, was about $1,800,000. More than half of that amount was a gift from Andrew Carnegie. Besides this Central Library there are about 20 branches and 75 substations scattered throughout the city. More than 3,000,000 books are loaned out by the public library each year.

An early printing press

Joseph Charless—editor of the first newspaper west of the Mississippi

THE NEWS IN PRINT

Home of the Missouri Gazette

J oseph Charless arrived by keelboat from Ohio with the announcement that he would soon start a weekly newspaper — the first one west of the Mississippi. St. Louis was then forty-four years old.

The *Missouri Gazette* was the name Charless gave to his eight-by-twelve inch newspaper. Since the news and advertising were to be in French and English, everyone in the community could read it. A year's subscription was $3 in money or $4 worth of country produce.

The *Missouri Gazette* office was a popular place for businessmen to meet and talk about politics. Often Indians would come by to look at a paper. Though few of them could read, they held a paper and turned the pages when others did.

Editor Charless ran a good paper but didn't make much money. This made him turn to other sources for income. He had such side jobs as stabling horses, taking in boarders, and recording sales of real estate.

Some of the news was very much like that you read in today's papers. There were articles about litter in the streets, muddy streets, the

163

Missouri Gazette

VOL. I.   TUESDAY, JULY 26, 1808   No. 3.

ST. LOUIS, LOUISIANA.

PRINTED BY JOSEPH CHARLESS,

Printer to the Territory.

Terms of Subscription for the
MISSOURI GAZETTE.

Three Dollars paid in advance.

Advertisements not exceeding a square, will be inserted one week for one dollar, and Fifty cents for every continuance, those of a greater length in proportion.

Advertisements sent to this Office, without specifying the time they are to be inserted, will be continued until forbid, and charged accordingly

LONDON, April 22.

Upon the subject of Sir John Duckworth's late cruize, we have been favored with the following extract of a letter from an officer belonging to the squadron, dated

"Cawsand Bay, April 18.

"Having run down the Bay of Biscay, and called off Capes Ortugal and Finisterre, and Lisbon, we arrived off Madeira, and found Sir Samuel Hood, laying in Funschall roads, where we remained for two days. On the morning of the 3d of February, his majesty's ship Comus, gave us intelligence of her having been chased two days before to the N. W. of Madeira, and it then became obvious that the destination of the French squadron was the West Indies, for which we proceeded with all expedition & made the islands of St. Lucia and Martinique in twenty one days. Off the east end of Martinique we saw six sail of the line; we cleared for action, and formed the line of battle, but, on exchanging signals we found instead of enemies ; it was Sir Alexander Cochrane, with his squadron, who was waiting to give that enemy a reception which we were in chase of, conceiving that he would take refuge in that port. Finding that his fleet was sufficient to cope with them in those seas, we passed all the Windward Islands, and anchored on the 16th of February in Bassaterre Roads, St. Kitts, where we remained only 18 hours, just long enough to take in water, but no provisions, nor even linen washed. We then proceeded to Saint Domingo, where it was supposed the enemy had proceeded for the purpose of landing troops; but on our arrival there we found no ships   After cruizing in the Mono Passage for seven or eight days, we made all dispatch for the coast of America, and arrived off the Chesepeake on the 11th March. We communicated with the Statira frigate, and found that our Ambassador, Mr. Rose, was at Washington for the last time, to determine whether it should be peace or war with England. *We* should have gone in, but the Yankies would not let us have a pilot, nor supply us with water and provisions, which forced us to be content to live upon half our usual allowance; they would not give us a single pint of water or a cabbage stock. We left the Eurydice, to bring us any intelligence that might occur as to peace or war with America, and quitted the inhospitable shores of America for the Western Islands, where we procured all we wanted, after a long and very anxious cruise. The Governor of Flores [a Portuguese,] came off to us, but not being able to give us any information, the Admiral thought it most expedient to proceed for England, where we arrived this morning, after having been three months at sea, and made a complete circuit of the Western and Atlantic Ocean, a journey of upwards of thirteen thousand miles."

We learn by other letters, that our squadron remained several days off the Chesepeake, and that the treatment it experienced was such as by no means to encourage the hopes of late entertained by many, of an amicably termination of our present negotiation with the United States. It is certain, that no article whatever of supply could be obtained by our admiral from the inhospitable and hostile Americans; and it follows of course, that the reparation offered by our government for the affair of the Chesepeake frigate was made in vain; although that circumstance alone, since so amply atoned for, was assigned by the President's proclamation as the motive for prohibiting all intercourse between the inhabitants and such British ships of war as might arrive in the American waters. Such conduct argues so hostile a determination in the government of the United States, that the general opinion expressed by the officers of our squadron, "that a war with America is inevitable," cannot be considered as founded upon weak or trivial grounds. We should have expected that Mr. Rose's mission would at least have procured for our squadron the rights of hospitality, if it did not effect a complete re-establishment of the former good understanding between the two countries; but we fear the Frenchified government of the United States has so far resigned itself to the baseful influence of the cabinet of the Thuilleries, that nothing but salutary chastisement will bring it to a due sense of the pernicious error into which its unnatural propensities have permitted it to be led. If America will have war with Great Britain, she will have herself only to blame for the consequences. It is our sincere wish to remain at peace with her, and our ministers, it is well known, have adopted every expedient short of comprising the honor, the dignity of the nation to avoid the extremity of warfare; but we are certainly not prepared to lay the honor and the essential interests of the empire at the feet of any junto upon earth. The blustering American demagogues may perhaps have founded some portion of their confidence upon the support of a certain party in this country; some of them, as we lately took occasion to remark, may derive hopes from the confiscation of property and the non-payment of debts; they may conceal from themselves their comparative impotence, by throwing their weight into the aggregate of the enemies of G. Britain; but a few short months of war would convince these politicions of the folly of measuring their puny strength with the colossal power of the British empire. *We* do not ourselves wish to be understood, as stating positively that a war with the United States is become inevitable; the door for amicable adjustment still remains open, and while it continues so, hopes of adjustment may not irrationally be indulged. But in whatever manner the negotiation may terminate, we shall have the consolation to re-

(See 4th Page.)

Republican Building—1873

An early Globe-Democrat *building*

bloody duels, so common then between well-known citizens, and the lack of police protection, as well as articles about the Louisiana Territory and its problems.

Twelve years after the *Missouri Gazette* began, Editor Charless sold it. The man who bought it kept it only eighteen months and then sold it to the oldest son of Charless who changed the name to the *Missouri Republic*. This paper later became the *St. Louis Republic*, a morning paper.

The *Daily Missouri Democrat,* direct forerunner of the *Globe-Democrat,* was founded by Francis P. Blair in 1852. Despite the name *Democrat,* it was actually for Republican causes. The day Abraham Lincoln was elected was good news for the paper because *The Democrat* had worked hard for his victory. President Lincoln said later that *The Democrat* was worth more to the Union cause "than a regiment of troops." St. Louis, at that time, was divided on the slavery question. Many people were for abolition, others were for the continuation of slavery, and still others wanted a compromise. The paper was a source of displeasure to the many Southern sympathizers living in St. Louis.

It was in 1875 that the *Globe* and the *Democrat* merged to become the *Globe-Democrat.*

The newspaper soon became known as a "big spender" because it paid high telegraph and cable rates to bring the news of the nation and world to St. Louis. The rival morning paper, the *St. Louis Republic,* was bought in 1919 under the then president and publisher E. Lansing Ray. Mr. Ray set forth the policy of the paper which you see today daily under the masthead: "The *Globe-Democrat* is an independent newspaper printing the news impartially, supporting what it believes to be right, and opposing what it believes to be wrong, without regard to party politics."

Today's *Globe,* under Publisher Richard Amberg, is known for its crusades, direct public appeal campaigns, and awards made to outstanding citizens.

There were twenty-one newspapers in St. Louis in 1854. Senator Thomas Hart Benton was an editor of the *St. Louis Enquirer* before his political career began. *The St. Louis Observer,* edited by Elijah P. Lovejoy, became famous because of its antislavery policy. When it was destroyed by a mob, the editors went to Alton and started a similar publication. It also was mobbed, and Editor Lovejoy was killed. The all-Negro town of Lovejoy, Illinois, was named for this courageous man.

Carl Schurz

The *Westliche Post*, a German language paper, had a strong influence on the opinions of the large German population. When Dr. Emil Preetorius became editor in 1864, the Germans were·strongly in favor of staying·in the Union. They hated slavery and spoke out against it. Another German-American, Carl Schurz, joined Preetorius as an editor on the *Post*. Schurz was nationally known by the time he reached St. Louis and was given credit for lining up the nation's million and a half German votes solidly for Abraham Lincoln. Schurz was highly respected in Missouri, as the leader of the Republican Party. He was United States Senator from Missouri from 1869 to 1875. Later, President Hayes appointed him Secretary of the Interior. Both Preetorius and Schurz played a big part in the life of a young Austrian whose name is still honored around the world—Joseph Pulitzer.

It was wartime in 1864 in Boston Harbor when seventeen-year-old Joseph slid quietly over the side of a sailing ship and made for shore. The ship was an immigrant boat filled with husky young immigrants who would serve as substitutes for citizens called to duty in the Union Army but unwilling to serve. Such citizens were excused on payment of a certain sum to the government. The boys didn't know the immigrant agent was getting bounty on them because the paper they had signed was written in English and they couldn't read it. Joseph had overheard him talking about the $500 he received for each recruit brought over. Joseph wanted to join the Army and fight slavery, but he did not want the agent to get the $500.

After swimming to shore, he made his way to New York, where he became a member of the Lincoln Cavalry. Joseph, knowing no English, had a difficult time getting along in the Army. In his eagerness to learn the language he often made the mistake of asking questions of his officers. For this he was teased and treated brutally; but, fortunately, the war was soon over. He returned to New York with little money and found jobs were scarce for ex-soldiers. A friend suggested that he go west to St. Louis.

Joseph Pulitzer arrived, cold and lonely, in East St. Louis with no money to ride the ferry across the river. Luckily for him, a fireman was late for work and Joseph got his job, shoveling coal for his passage to St. Louis.

Joseph learned about the city as a laborer on the docks and steamboats, as a hostler at Benton Barracks, and as a messenger for a

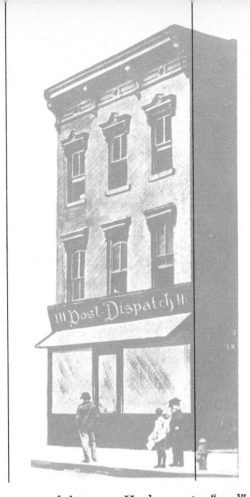

Joseph Pulitzer

group of lawyers. He began to "read" law with one of them. In addition he spent hours in the Mercantile Library studying history, mathematics, philosophy, geography, literature, and science. It was here he met Professor Thomas Davidson, a young Scottish school teacher, who was to become a lifelong friend. Here also he met Schurz and Preetorius. In spite of Pulitzer's shabby, scrawny appearance, his keen mind impressed them, and they offered him a job as a reporter on the *Westliche Post.* This was a job that really suited his inquisitive mind. He began a fearless, never-satisfied crusade for better news, more news, accurate news, and a wider variety of news. No detail was too small; no hour too late to work. He was all over town gathering news.

He built up the *Post* until he was named publisher. He also became part owner. The other owners were jealous and frightened of his power and pressured him to sell his share. Pulitzer gave in. His years of overwork had given him bad headaches and the doctors had warned him he must rest. At twenty-five he was a rich man with $30,000.

Pulitzer went back to Europe to visit his family. After months of traveling there and in the United States, he was still undecided about his future. While in Washington, D. C., he

courted and married Kate Davis, who thoroughly approved of Pulitzer's sharp mind, fine appearance, and polished manners.

After the honeymoon, Pulitzer brought his bride back to St. Louis. He was just in time to buy the old *St. Louis Dispatch* cheaply. A few days later he bought the *St. Louis Post* and joined the two papers to make the *St. Louis Post-Dispatch.* He declared that the new paper would "serve no party but the people."

Pulitzer later moved with his wife and family to New York where he bought the *New York World* and made it a great paper. Always a tireless worker, he suffered from eye trouble and eventually went blind. This didn't stop him from demanding the best from his reporters and editors; his high standards of journalism live on today.

Pulitzer established the Columbia University School of Journalism and the Pulitzer Prize. The prizes are given annually in a number of literary and journalistic categories for the outstanding work that will advance the cause of democracy.

Today our afternoon newspaper, the *St. Louis Post-Dispatch,* is edited by Pulitzer's grandson, who continues the traditions of journalistic excellence established by Joseph Pulitzer — Father of Modern Journalism.

THE Argus
AND American

Mrs. Nannie Mitchell-Turner
at the annual Argus dinner

The Saint Louis Argus

Two years before World War I began, the *Saint Louis Argus*, a five column tabloid-size newspaper, was registered at the United States Post Office. The paper's name came from Greek mythology. Argus was a creature with one hundred eyes which were never all closed at the same time.

From the very beginning, the Mitchell family has operated the newspaper. It was started by two brothers, Joseph and William Mitchell. Originally they thought it would be a trade paper for their insurance company, but decided it would give greater service as a regular newspaper. *The Argus*, by 1914 a regular size newspaper, entered into many civic and political fights. It sponsored the Citizen's Liberty League — the first important political movement of Negro St. Louisans. It helped Negroes

Executive Editor Howard Woods and Governor Dalton looking over some facts about the St. Louis Argus

Publisher Frank Mitchell announcing the Argus *awardees*

obtain more jobs in the Fire and Police Departments and increased their representation in the Legislature.

Mr. Joseph (J.E.) Mitchell, managing editor, was a fighter for better schools, educational opportunities, and full civil rights for Negro Americans. He was a presidential elector during the Roosevelt Administration and was a personal acquaintance of President Harry S. Truman. He served on the Missouri State Board of Education, was a YMCA pioneer, and received awards from Lincoln University, the Urban League, and the National Newspaper Publishers Association for the paper's contribution to journalism. His wife, Mrs. Edwina Mitchell, was women's page editor for some years.

William Mitchell, the older brother, was business manager until his death in 1945. His wife, now Mrs. Nannie Mitchell-Turner, carried on his role as business manager. Later she became president and treasurer of the Argus Publishing Company. Under her presidency, *The Argus* moved from its Market Street address to a new, modern plant at 4595 Easton and started the *Argus* Awards Dinner. This annual affair recognizes outstanding citizens and groups from all walks of life. Mrs. Turner's son, Frank Mitchell, Sr., became the first publisher. Direct-

ing the writing end of the weekly is executive editor, Howard B. Woods, a member of President Johnson's Committee on Equal Employment Opportunity.

The Argus, now fifty-two years old, is read weekly by thousands of subscribers in St. Louis and in the large cities throughout the nation. A new elementary school now bears the name of Joseph and William Mitchell.

The Saint Louis American

The St. Louis American, another weekly, came into being in 1928. It was the brainchild of three men: Dick Kent, owner of a fleet of taxicabs and the St. Louis Giants Baseball team; Charlie Turpin, leading politician and first Negro constable in St. Louis; and N. B. Young, Yale-trained lawyer and historian.

The American, not pulling any punches, has had a strong editorial policy from the beginning. It has taken a forthright policy towards critical issues in the community. In the thirties *The American* initiated a "Buy where you can work" campaign that resulted in the increased employment of Negroes in sales positions.

Born in a political boom year, with predictions that it would not last, *The American* lives on. Under the leadership of N. A. Sweets, editor and publisher, it has proved that with hard work it can survive.

*In a corner of this warehouse the
Monsanto Company was founded in 1901.*

In the
Working
World

BEGINNING WITH SACCHARIN

In 1899 John Francis Queeny had $6000 and a job with a leading St. Louis drug company, Meyer Brothers. With the money — his life savings — he set up a small sulphur plant across the river in East St. Louis. On its opening day the plant burned to the ground.

Luckily Queeny had kept his job, and soon he had another idea. At that time anyone who wanted the chemical sweetener, saccharin, had to buy it from Germany. Meyer Brothers needed a great deal of it, and Queeny, as buyer for the company, did the ordering. But he saw no reason why saccharin should not be made right here in St. Louis.

In two years Queeny saved up $1,500. He got a local soft drink company and others to put up $3,500 more. In 1901 he opened a small chemical works in a wooden building at 1812 South Second Street. He called it Monsanto for his wife, Olga Monsanto Queeny, the daughter of a Spanish engineer.

Three people worked in the little one-room plant — Queeny, a young Swiss chemist named Louis Veillon, and one helper. From a chemical compound that Queeny got from Germany they made the finished product — saccharin.

After several hard years, the little company seemed about to make money. Then the German manufacturers began to worry about losing their American customers to Monsanto. When they decided to cut down the amount of the compound they sold to Queeny, he refused to buy from them. The fight was on.

Queeny found that he could purchase the needed chemical in Switzerland. The Germans fought back by putting up a saccharin plant of their own in New Jersey. Then, to force Monsanto out of business, they sold their product for less than it cost to make it. The price of saccharin went down from $6 to 60 cents a pound.

Monsanto was not rich enough to win this price war. By 1904 Queeny had only $204, but he did not give up. Off he went to Germany to find out how to make vanillin — the substance in vanilla that gives it its pleasant smell. There he found someone who could help him — a young Swiss student named Gaston DuBois. DuBois agreed to come back to America with Queeny. Soon Monsanto was making vanillin, as well as other products. Moreover, new processes of manufacturing saccharin enabled Monsanto to sell the product as cheaply as the Germans did and still make money. After a three-year fight Queeny and Monsanto won out.

When World War I broke out in 1914, Monsanto was doing a good business. But, like other American manufacturers, it bought its raw materials from Europe. The war cut off the supply. A drug used in the treatment of influenza was the first to give out. Monsanto learned how to make it and other needed drugs from raw materials found in the United States.

After World War I, Monsanto increased the number of its products; and when World War II began, it was well prepared to produce important materials for weapons, foods, clothing, and drugs. It helped build and operate

Monsanto today

nine government plants to supply chemicals needed in warfare. The company made no profit from any of its government projects. But not until after the war did people hear about Monsanto's most important service — work in the company's laboratories had helped pave the way for the atom bomb. When the war was over, Monsanto helped in the peace-time use of atomic energy.

In 1957 Monsanto moved its general offices and some of its research departments from their first location to a large stretch of land at

Lindbergh and Olive Street roads in **Creve Coeur**. There researchers experiment on many Monsanto products. Visitors touring the Creve Coeur buildings may be startled to see these researchers weighing pans of biscuits and cake to test Monsanto products used in making baking powder. They also see rows of automatic washers cleaning clothes that have been soiled with measured amounts of dirt, grease, and stains; through this procedure products used in making detergents and textiles are perfected.

Through the years, led by John Queeny and later by his son Edgar Queeny, Monsanto has grown steadily. Today it operates forty plants in the United States with some 35,000 employees and has manufacturing interests in fifteen foreign countries, employing 10,000 more. Although the first product, saccharin, is still an important one, thousands of chemicals, plastics, and other products have been added. Monsanto is the largest manufacturer of aspirin ingredients in the world. Four of Monsanto's plants are still in the St. Louis area — among them the Queeny plant on South Second Street, where the Monsanto story began.

Brewing Is BIG BUSINESS

Bavarian Brewery

In 1860 the average St. Louisan drank 658 glasses of beer per year. Many of the German immigrants drank much more than this, but it was the French who introduced beer to St. Louis.

The St. Vrain's brewery opened in 1810 and burned to the ground two years later. But other breweries soon replaced it. Until 1840 beer had been very strong-tasting, but in that year the Lemp Brewery opened and made the first mild-tasting beer (lager), a type popular in Germany. Next door to the Lemp Brewery was a saloon which became a favorite meeting place of businessmen.

St. Louis had forty breweries, when Eberhard Anheuser, who had a soap factory, bought the Bavarian Brewery. He ran both businesses for eight years, and then gave up soap manufacturing. Anheuser's pretty blond daughter, Lily, found a young brewery supply store operator named Adolphus Busch very much to her liking. Lily's sister Anna and Adolphus's brother also fell in love. The couples were married in a double wedding on the eve of the Civil War. After service in the Union Army, Adolphus returned to St. Louis and joined his father-in-law in the business. The brewery was renamed Anheuser-Busch in 1879.

Adolphus Busch and his good friend Carl Conrad, who had come from the town of Budweis in Bavaria, concocted a recipe for a new light lager beer. The secret was in the Bohemian hops and brewer's rice. The beer was produced during the cold months and kept in natural caves along the Mississippi River such as the old Cherokee Cave at Seventh and Cherokee streets and the Mammoth Cave at Wisconsin and Wyoming streets. The brew was packed in ice cut the previous winter from the river, and in the summer it was brought out cool to refresh the thirsty citizens. The large German population made beer gardens, parks, and caves very popular outing spots in the city. The brewery later opened a glass bottle factory and developed refrigerated railroad cars to haul beer to distant markets and to international fame.

Perhaps on a trip to Grant's Farm you have seen the amazing Clydesdale horses. The eight-horse draft teams have toured the country and are seen on television commercials as they burst through the gate of the Bauernhof complete with wagon and a sprightly driver. These horses weigh about two thousand pounds each. They are very intelligent and respond to commands quickly. They remind us of the days when beer was delivered to dealers by horse and wagon.

Prohibition was a hard blow for all the breweries, but the Busch family produced other products such as soft drinks, a near beer beverage, and baker's yeast. When the Prohibition Era closed, the Anheuser-Busch Company again swung into full production of beer, and it started other products. One of these was the syrup you may have used on your pancakes. Others are corn products, frozen eggs, industrial starches, baking powder, and vitamin complexes.

174

Today, under the leadership of August A. Busch, Jr., the brewery here is the largest in the world; it covers 70 city blocks near the banks of the Mississippi River. There are branch breweries in Newark, New Jersey; in Los Angeles, California; and in Tampa, Florida.

Mr. Busch does not limit his leadership to the beer industry. He supports St. Louis community organizations. When it appeared that the St. Louis Symphony, second oldest in the country, would have to give up, his company made a generous contribution to keep it going. Again in 1953, when St. Louis was about to lose its baseball team, the St. Louis Cardinals, the Busch firm bought the team. Busch also served as the first president of Civic Progress, Incorporated, and president of the St. Louis Bicentennial Celebration.

August A. Busch, Jr.

The amazing Clydesdale horses moving along at a fast clip

The Falstaff Brewing Corporation can claim linkage with a long line of brewers beginning with the Griesedieck family, which operated a brewery in Germany as early as the 1700's. Anton Griesedieck opened a brewery in St. Louis in 1870. Joseph Griesedieck began working there as a boy and learned to be a brewmaster. In 1891 he was co-founder of the National Brewery here. A little later his son Alvin joined him when he founded the Griesedieck Beverage Company. They had a bad time during the prohibition era, but the company made soda and processed ham and bacon. After the repeal, Falstaff was able to take over a second plant, and the business has been zooming ever since with plants in San Jose, California; in Galveston and El Paso, Texas; in Omaha, Nebraska; and in Fort Wayne, Indiana. The central laboratory here has done what was long thought impossible. The company produced identical beer at plants all over the country.

The Carling Brewing Company, which ranks fourth in production in the nation today, came to this area when it took over the Griesedieck Western assets in Belleville and St. Louis in 1954. It now has a modern brewery in Belleville and helps to make St. Louis the nation's third largest brewing center.

*The first
Poro hair products
were made here.*

BLAZING
THE
TRAIL

Annie Turnbo loved to braid and twist the hair of her sisters and friends into attractive styles. Her parents had died when she was a child, and she lived with her older brothers and sisters in Metropolis, Illinois. Annie was sickly during her teens and was unable to work, play, or attend school, but this left plenty of time for dreaming. Her dream was to make a product that would enhance the beauty of the Negro woman's hair. At first, she could only dream, but when her health improved she returned to finish high school. Here she studied chemistry so that she could learn more about hair preparations. She experimented and finally developed a preparation which she called "Wonderful Hair Grower."

In 1900 Miss Turnbo moved with her older sister to Lovejoy, Illinois, where she launched her little business in the rear room of a small frame building. People were skeptical at first about the hair grower and scalp treatments she offered. Gradually customers increased;

three assistants were hired and trained in the new methods of beauty culture. Annie's customers were happy with the results. The fame of her hair preparations and methods of teaching spread to St. Louis.

St. Louis was making ready for the World's Fair. It was a good time to expand her business. She located at 2223 Market Street and began to advertise her products by going from house to house asking women to let her treat their hair and scalp. When competitors began to imitate her products, she knew that she had become successful. This led her to copyright her trade name—Poro.

Miss Turnbo, now Mrs. Malone, soon found her products were being used throughout the United States and in other countries. To meet the demand she planned a large, modern building that would house both the business and a beauty college. In 1918 the million-dollar Poro College was opened at 4300 St. Ferdinand Street. Here beauty operators were trained.

She chose the land near several schools to inspire the thousands of school children who passed by everyday.

Great artists — Marian Anderson, Roland Hayes, Ethel Waters, and many others — appeared on the stage of the Poro College auditorium. A roof garden atop the building was enjoyed by many St. Louisans. The west annex, which opened in 1920, was a factory which produced hair and cosmetic preparations. Two hundred employees worked there and in the large mail order department.

Deeply religious all her life, Mrs. Malone led the students and employees in a daily chapel service. Orchestras, fancy needlework clubs, and culture groups were organized to help people make better use of their leisure time.

By 1925 Mrs. Malone was a millionaire. She made substantial gifts to the Y.M.C.A., Howard University, and the St. Louis Colored Orphans' Home.

Although Mrs. Malone extended the Poro operation to Chicago and made Chicago her permanent home, she could always be found in St. Louis every fourth Sunday in May. This was the day of the May Day Parade. The Parade is still held annually to raise funds for the Orphans' Home at 2612 Goode Avenue. People line the streets to see the floats, bands, drum and bugle corps, marching Scouts, and decorated cars. The Home, for which she worked so hard all her life, was later renamed the Annie Malone Children's Home.

Annie Turnbo Malone died at the age of 87, but her business still flourishes in Chicago. Her memory lives on in the Hall of Fame in Washington, D. C., the Poro Building, a maternity ward at Barnes Hospital, and a host of Poro clubs and shops throughout the country.

Annie Turnbo Malone

Building formerly occupied by Poro College, 4300 St. Ferdinand.

The Annie Malone Children's Home

MAYORS OF ST. LOUIS

Mayors	Years
William Carr Lane	1823-1828
Daniel D. Page	1829-1832
Samuel Merry	1833-1834
Col. John F. Darby	1835-1837
William Carr Lane	1838-1839
John F. Dory	1840
John D. Daggett	1841
George Maguire	1842
John M. Wimer	1843
Bernard Pratte	1844-1845
Peter G. Camden	1846
Bryan Mullanphy	1847
John M. Krum	1848
James G. Barry	1849
Luther M. Kennett	1850-1852
John How	1853-1854
Washington King	1855-1856
John M. Wimer	1857
Oliver D. Filley	1858-1860
Daniel G. Taylor	1861-1862
Chauncey I. Filley	1863
James S. Thomas	1864-1868
Nathan Cole	1869-1870
Joseph Brown	1871-1874
Arthur B. Barret (Died in Office)	1875
James H. Britton	1875
Henry Overstolz	1876-1881
William L. Ewing	1881-1885
David R. Francis	1885-1889
Edward A. Noonan	1889-1893
Cyrus P. Walbridge	1893-1897
Henry Ziegenhein	1897-1901
Rolla Wells	1901-1909
Frederick H. Kreismann	1909-1913
Henry Kiel	1913-1925
Victor J. Miller	1925-1933
Bernard F. Dickmann	1933-1941
William Dee Becker (Died in Office)	1941-1943
Aloys P. Kaufmann	1943-1949
Joseph M. Darst	1949-1953
Raymond R. Tucker	1953

Through
the
Years

1764	*Pierre Laclede and Auguste Chouteau chose the site for St. Louis on the west side of the river and, with thirty men, began building the first houses on February 15, 1764.*
	The first child was born in St. Louis; he was named Jean B. Guion.
1765	*On July 17 Louis St. Ange de Bellerive, with about fifty men, moved to St. Louis. St. Ange established the capital of Upper Louisiana here.*
1766	*The first marriage ceremony was performed in the town.*
1767	*Carondelet was established.*
1770	*The first Spanish governor, Don Pedro Piernas, arrived in St. Louis and took charge under a treaty in which France gave Spain that part of the Mississippi Valley west of the river.*
1774	*The first school on record, a private school for boys, was established by Jean Baptiste Trudeau.*

1775	*The building of the Catholic cathedral was begun.*
1779	*A rowboat ferry service across the river was started.*
	English and Indians attacked the town. Several settlers were killed.
1780	*The Indians attacked again.*
1800	*Spain ceded Louisiana back to France.*
1803	*The United States purchased Louisiana from France on April 30.*
	The population was about seven hundred whites and four hundred slaves.
1804	*March 10 was the Day of the Three Flags (Spanish, French, and United States) when Upper Louisiana was officially transferred to the United States.*
	The Lewis and Clark Expedition left St. Louis to explore the upper Mississippi and Missouri rivers.
	The first English-language school was started.

1808 The Missouri Gazette, *the first paper west of the Mississippi, began publication.*

A Post Office was established (rates were about fifty cents a sheet for more than 450 miles, postage payable in advance; stamps were not used).

1809 *The town of St. Louis was incorporated. The boundaries were the river on the east, Mill Creek (now Poplar Street) on the south, Seventh Street on the west, and Roy's Tower (just north of Franklin Avenue) on the north.*

The population was about one thousand.

The first dancing school was opened.

1810 *The first duel was fought on Bloody Island.*

1811 *The Missouri Fur Company was organized by Chouteau and others.*

The first manufacturing plant began operations; it used water power from Chouteau's Pond.

A severe earthquake shook St. Louis.

1812 *The Territory of Louisiana was renamed the Territory of Missouri, with William Clark as governor.*

1813 *The Bank of St. Louis was incorporated, the first authorized to issue bank notes.*

Prior to this, trade had been carried on by barter; furs, other supplies, and foreign coins were the means of exchange.

1815 *Territorial legislators established a Board of School Trustees for St. Louis. They were William Clark, William C. Carr, and T. H. Benton.*

1817 *The first steamboat, the* General Pike, *landed at the levee.*

The first courthouse was built.

1821 *Missouri was admitted as a state under the Missouri Compromise.*

The first Missouri Constitutional Convention and the first legislature met in St. Louis.

The first sidewalks were laid.

The first directory of St. Louis was published, giving the population as 5,500.

The first Methodist church was built.

Volunteer fire companies were organized.

1822 *The town of St. Louis became the City of St. Louis.*

1823 *A law was passed to punish careless driving through the streets.*

1824 *The first Presbyterian church was built.*

1825 *General Lafayette visited the city as a guest of Chouteau.*

The first Episcopal church was built.

1826 *Fort San Carlos at Fourth and Walnut streets and Fort Bellefontaine on the Missouri River were abandoned.*

Jefferson Barracks was established.

1828 *Mullanphy Hospital was founded at Third and Spruce streets.*

A steam ferry across the river was started.

1829 *St. Louis University, founded in 1818, was incorporated and opened at Ninth and Washington streets.*

1830   *The first water reservoir and pipes were installed.*

1832   *Carondelet was incorporated.*

Asiatic cholera killed over four hundred people in St. Louis.

1833   *Public schools were started when the first Board of Education was formed.*

1834   *The present Old Cathedral was built.*

1835   *The common seal of the city was adopted.*

1836   *A railroad convention was held in St. Louis.*

1837   *The St. Louis Gaslight Company was incorporated with right to sell gas for fifty years in city and suburbs.*

1838   *The St. Louis Medical Society was founded.*

The first public school was opened.

Six hundred German Lutherans landed in St. Louis and moved to Perry County, Missouri, where they founded Concordia Seminary.

1840   *The brewing of beer began in St. Louis.*

1841   *The city limits extended to Eighteenth Street.*

1842   *The first steamboat was built in the city.*

1843   *The city established a health department.*

1844   *Lafayette Park was purchased by the city.*

1846   *St. Louis military units took part in the Mexican War.*

Mercantile Library was incorporated.

The Police department was organized with a day force of one lieutenant and seven privates, and a night force of six lieutenants and forty-two privates.

1847   *The City Hospital was opened.*

Bellefontaine Cemetery was incorporated.

The first artificial gas was manufactured and piped to homes for lighting.

1848   *The Post Office site at Eighth and Olive was chosen.*

The first telegraph line was built to St. Louis from the East.

1849   *St. Louis had three great disasters: a river flood, a cholera epidemic, and a great fire that destroyed the central part of the city and twenty-three steamboats.*

Concordia Seminary was moved to St. Louis.

1850   *Public schools become free, tax-supported institutions. Prior to this date they were financed by tuition or rentals from Board owned properties.*

The first public sewer was built.

1851   *The Germans organized their first gymnastic society.*

Jenny Lind arrived in St. Louis for five concerts at the Old Salt Theater.

1853   *Eliot Seminary, later Washington University, was incorporated.*

Central High School was opened with a principal, four teachers, and seventy pupils.

181

1855 The city limits were extended west of Grand.

The first train on the Pacific Railroad broke through a bridge over the Gasconade River, killing many important St. Louisans.

1856 The United States Supreme Court ruled against Dred Scott in his trial for freedom.

1857 A city fire department was organized.

The name of Eliot Seminary was changed to Washington University.

1858 Shaw's Garden was opened to the public by Henry Shaw.

The first overland mail from California reached city after journey of twenty-four days.

1859 Horse cars began operating.

1860 The public library was established at Fifth and Olive streets.

1861 The Civil War began. A convention was held in St. Louis to consider secession; it voted for the Union.

1862 The Courthouse was finished at Broadway and Market streets.

1864 The insane asylum was opened.

1866 The Missouri Historical Society was organized.

The first schools for Negroes were opened by the Board of Education.

1867 Eads Bridge was begun.

The first mounted police force was organized.

1868 The monument to Thomas Hart Benton in Lafayette Park was unveiled.

1869 Tower Grove Park was given to city by Henry Shaw.

1870 Carondelet was annexed by St. Louis.

1872 St. Paul's African Methodist Episcopal church was erected at Lewton and Ewing — the first church built by and for Negroes west of the Mississippi.

1873 Susan Blow opened the first public school kindergarten in Des Peres School.

1874 Eads Bridge was dedicated. The first train from the east entered St. Louis.

Forest Park was bought by the city.

1875 Sumner High School opened at Eleventh and Spruce.

1876 The first telephone was exhibited in St. Louis.

1877 The first Negro teachers were employed by the Board of Education.

1878 The first Veiled Prophet Parade and Ball were held.

The first telephone service was set up.

1884 Electricity was used for the first time.

1887 *Electric street cars were introduced.*

1894 *Union Station, on Eighteenth and Market streets, was opened.*

1896 *A tornado on May 27 wrecked many buildings, killing 306, and injuring hundreds.*

1898 *Many St. Louisans enlisted for the Spanish-American War.*

1902 *There were 176 automobiles in St. Louis.*

1904 *The World's Fair was held in St. Louis.*

The Olympic Games were held at Francis Field.

1905 *The world's first drive-in service station was built on Theresa near Market Street.*

1908 *The Free Bridge was built south of Eads Bridge. (It was later named MacArthur Bridge.)*

1909 *The first airplane flight in St. Louis was made.*

The Coliseum was built.

1911 *The Municipal Courts building was finished.*

The world's first airmail flown was from Kinloch Park to Fairgrounds Park.

1913 *The St. Louis Zoo was established. Henry Kiel was elected Mayor.*

1914 *The Federal Reserve Bank of St. Louis opened.*

1916 *The Democratic National Convention meeting at the Coliseum nominated Woodrow Wilson.*

1919 *The American Legion and the League of Women Voters were founded here.*

Municipal Opera began with the performance of Robin Hood.

1920 *Radio broadcasting began.*

1923 *The city voted an $87,000,000 bond issue to widen streets, enclose the River Des Peres, open the Twelfth Street Plaza, and build Civil Courts building, Kiel Auditorium, and other public buildings.*

1924 *Scottish Rite Cathedral was finished.*

1925 *KMOX became the first St. Louis radio station to have continuous evening broadcasting.*

1926 *The Cardinals won their first National League pennant and the World's Series.*

Southwestern Bell Telephone Company Building (369 feet tall) was completed.

Queen Marie of Rumania visited St. Louis.

1927   *Charles A. Lindbergh made his successful flight from New York to Paris non-stop.*

The city's second big tornado struck on September 29; many buildings were destroyed, and 72 were killed.

Streets were lighted by electricity for the first time; old gas lamps were removed.

1928   *New Public School Stadium was opened.*

The city acquired Lambert Field.

1930   *The Old Courthouse was abandoned.*

The old Grand National Bank was robbed of $1,000,000.

1934   *Kiel Municipal Auditorium was opened.*

Congress created the Territorial Expansion Memorial Commission to plan a riverfront memorial.

1935   *The city voted $7,500,000 in bonds for the riverfront memorial and prepared to buy and clear forty blocks downtown.*

1936   *The Eugene Field Museum was opened.*

1937   *The last link in the Express Highway (now Daniel Boone) was completed.*

1939   *The McDonnell Aircraft Corporation started as a two-man concern.*

1940   *A plan for getting rid of smoke was put into operation.*

1941   *Production started at the St. Louis Ordnance Plant, which made 40% of small arms ammunition fired by American troops in World War II.*

There was severe rationing of food and materials.

1942   *The St. Louis area became a wartime arsenal.*

1943   *Mayor William Dee Becker and nine others were killed in a glider crash at Lambert Field. Aloys P. Kaufman became Mayor.*

Dr. Edward A. Doisy, St. Louis University biochemist, won the Nobel Prize.

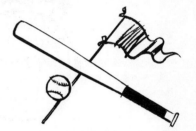

1944   *The Browns won the American League pennant, then lost to the Cardinals in the only all-St. Louis World's Series.*

1945   *Robert E. Hannegan was the first St. Louisan to become Postmaster General.*

1946   *Archbishop Glennon was made a Cardinal.*

Jefferson Barracks was de-activated after 120 years as a military post.

John W. Snyder was the first St. Louisan to become the United States Secretary of the Treasury.

1947   *St. Louis became the first large city to enforce a standard clean restaurant ordinance.*

1948   *The Saarinen design, with a 630 foot-high arch, was picked for the riverfront memorial.*

1949 *Dr. Edward L. Grant became the first Negro on the Board of Education.*

Joseph M. Darst was elected Mayor.

1950 *The $40,000,000 Chain of Rocks canal and locks was built near Granite City.*

The Urban Redevelopment Corporation of St. Louis was formed to develop a slum clearance program for middle-income housing.

1951 *The new $11,000,000 Veterans Memorial Bridge opened.*

1953 *August A. Busch Jr. bought the Cardinals for $3,750,000 from Fred Saigh.*

The St. Louis Browns transferred to Baltimore.

Raymond Tucker, a former public school student, was elected Mayor.

1954 *The new air terminal was built at Lambert-St. Louis Airport.*

1955 *St. Louisans approved a $110,639,000 bond issue for public improvements, including streets, zoo, fire department, hospitals, expressways, parks and playgrounds, street lighting, and public buildings.*

The Hawks, a professional basketball team, was brought to St. Louis.

1956 *The Mid-America Jubilee was staged on the riverfront.*

1959 *A 50,000 seat sports stadium was proposed for the riverfront.*

The third big tornado struck the city; twenty-one were killed and hundreds were injured.

1960 *The Plaza Apartments opened, St. Louis's first urban renewal project. Most of Mill Creek Valley area was torn down.*

1961 *Plans for the Gateway Arch were completed and work begun.*

1962 *St. Louis voters a p p r o v e d a $14,986,000 bond issue for city improvements and a $23,900,000 bond issue for schools.*

Voters approved a proposal to start the St. Louis-St. Louis County Junior College District.

1963 *The Bi-State Development Agency took over all transit lines.*

The Planetarium was opened.

1964 *President Johnson opened the city's Bicentennial Celebration.*

The
Names
of
St. Louis
Public
Schools

Presidents of the United States of America

1 CLEVELAND HIGH SCHOOL
   4352 Louisiana Avenue — opened 1915.
   Named for: Grover Cleveland, twenty-
   second and twenty-fourth President.

2 McKINLEY HIGH SCHOOL
   2156 Russell Boulevard — opened 1904.
   Named for: William McKinley,
   twenty-fifth President.

3 ROOSEVELT HIGH SCHOOL
   3230 Hartford Street — opened 1925.
   Named for: Theodore Roosevelt,
   twenty-sixth President.

4 ADAMS ELEMENTARY SCHOOL
   1311 Tower Grove — opened 1878.
   Named for: John and John Quincy Adams,
   second and sixth Presidents.

5 GARFIELD ELEMENTARY SCHOOL
   2612 Wyoming Street — opened 1937.
   Named for: James A. Garfield,
   twentieth President.

6 GRANT ELEMENTARY SCHOOL
   3009 Pennsylvania Avenue — opened 1893.
   Named for: Ulysses S. Grant,
   eighteenth President.

7 HARRISON ELEMENTARY SCHOOL
   4163 Green Lea Place — opened 1896.
   Named for: Benjamin Harrison,
   twenty-third President.

8 JACKSON ELEMENTARY SCHOOL
   1632 Hogan Street — opened 1898.
   Named for: Andrew Jackson,
   seventh President.

9 JEFFERSON ELEMENTARY SCHOOL
   1301 Hogan Street — opened 1959.
   Named for: Thomas Jefferson,
   third President.

10 MADISON ELEMENTARY SCHOOL
   1118 South Seventh Street — opened 1911.
   Named for: James Madison,
   fourth President.

11 MONROE ELEMENTARY SCHOOL
3641 Missouri Avenue — opened 1899.
Named for: James Monroe, fifth President.

12 WASHINGTON ELEMENTARY SCHOOL
1130 North Euclid — opened 1956.
Named for: George Washington, first President.

Statesmen/Lawyers/Government Service

1 SUMNER HIGH SCHOOL
4248 West Cottage Avenue — opened 1910.
Named for: Charles Sumner, United States Senator; fought for Negro rights.

2 BENTON ELEMENTARY SCHOOL
2847 North Kingshighway Boulevard — opened 1894.
Named for: Thomas Hart Benton, Missouri lawyer and statesman; served for thirty years in United States Senate.

3 BLAIR ELEMENTARY SCHOOL
2708 North Twenty-second Street — opened 1882.
Named for: Frank P. Blair, lawyer, soldier, Republican newspaper man, and politician.

4 BLOW ELEMENTARY SCHOOL
516 Loughborough Avenue — opened 1903.
Named for: Henry T. Blow, United States Congressman and Commissioner to South American countries; father of Susan Blow.

5 CARR LANE ELEMENTARY SCHOOL
1004 North Jefferson — opened 1959.
Named for: William Carr Lane, first mayor of St. Louis.

6 CLAY ELEMENTARY SCHOOL
3820 North Fourteenth Street — opened 1905.
Named for: Henry Clay, American statesman and orator.

7 CLINTON ELEMENTARY SCHOOL
1224 Grattan Street — opened 1940.
Named for: George Clinton, statesman, Vice President 1804-1812.

8 FRANKLIN SCHOOL
814 North Nineteenth Street — opened 1909.
Named for: Benjamin Franklin, printer and publisher; member of committee which drafted the Declaration of Independence; also one of the signers; member of the Constitutional Convention, 1787.

9 GRATIOT ELEMENTARY SCHOOL
1615 Hampton Avenue — opened 1882.
Named for: Charles Gratiot, first presiding judge (1804) of the Court of Quarter Sessions, Louisiana Territory, District of St. Louis.

10 HAMILTON ELEMENTARY SCHOOL
5819 Westminster Place — opened 1917.
Named for: Alexander Hamilton, first Secretary of the Treasury.

11 HENRY ELEMENTARY SCHOOL
1220 North Tenth Street — opened 1906.
Named for: Patrick Henry, American orator and patriot.

12 LAFAYETTE ELEMENTARY SCHOOL
815 Ann Avenue — opened 1907.
Named for: Marie Jean Paul Lafayette, French general and statesman; served our country during the Revolutionary War.

13 LANGSTON ELEMENTARY SCHOOL
5511 Wabada Avenue — opened 1964
Named for: John Mercer Langston of Virginia and Arthur D. Langston. John Langston received A.B. and law degree from Oberlin College before Civil War; only Negro congressman from Virginia in fifty-third Congress; organized law school and acting president, Howard University; U. S. Minister to Haiti; president, Virginia Normal School. Arthur Langston (son of John) teacher in St. Louis Public Schools from 1877 to his retirement as principal of Dessalines School.

14 MARSHALL ELEMENTARY SCHOOL
4342 Aldine Avenue — opened 1900.
Named for: John Marshall, Chief Justice, United States Supreme Court for thirty-four years.

15 WEBSTER ELEMENTARY SCHOOL
2127 North Eleventh Street — opened 1906.
Named for: Daniel Webster, statesman and orator.

16 WOERNER ELEMENTARY SCHOOL
6131 Leona Street — opened 1931.
Named for: J. Gabriel Woerner, newspaperman, lawyer, judge, and Missouri Senator.

Military Leaders

1 ATTUCKS ELEMENTARY SCHOOL
2022 Papin Street — opened 1949.
Named for: Crispus Attucks, born a slave in Farmington, Massachusetts; leader of a band of American patriots; first man to fall in the Boston Massacre.

2 DESSALINES ELEMENTARY SCHOOL
1745 Hadley Street — opened 1871, reconstructed 1904.
Named for: Jean Jacques Dessalines, general under Toussaint L'Ouverture; fought to free Haiti.

3 DEWEY ELEMENTARY SCHOOL
6746 Clayton Avenue — opened 1917.
Named for: George Dewey, admiral of the American Far Eastern fleet and hero of the Spanish American War.

4 FARRAGUT ELEMENTARY SCHOOL
4025 Sullivan Avenue — opened 1905.
Named for: David G. Farragut, American naval commander in the Civil War.

5 L'OUVERTURE ELEMENTARY SCHOOL
3021 Hickory Street — opened 1950.
Named for: Toussaint L'Ouverture. Haitian; led fight to eliminate slave trade.

6 LYON ELEMENTARY SCHOOL
7417 Vermont — opened 1909.
Named for: Nathaniel Lyon, American Union general; captured Camp Jackson here in the Civil War.

7 PRUITT ELEMENTARY SCHOOL
1212 N. Twenty-second Street — opened 1955.
Named for: Wendell O. Pruitt, graduate of Sumner High School; Air Force Captain decorated for distinguished service; member of 332nd Fighter Group and the 99th Squadron.

8 SHERMAN ELEMENTARY SCHOOL
3942 Flad Avenue — opened 1898.
Named for: William Tecumseh Sherman, Civil War general; seized Atlanta; lived in St. Louis before and after the Civil War.

9 SIGEL ELEMENTARY SCHOOL
2050 Allen Avenue — opened 1906.
Named for: Franz Sigel, German-American general in the Civil War; fought at battle of Camp Jackson in St. Louis.

Founders/Explorers/Promoters

1 CHARLESS ELEMENTARY SCHOOL
2226 Shenandoah Avenue — opened 1895.
Named for: Joseph Charless, Jr., promoter of welfare in St. Louis.

2 CHOUTEAU ELEMENTARY SCHOOL
1306 South Ewing — opened 1894.
Named for: Auguste Chouteau, co-founder of St. Louis; leading citizen.

3 CLARK ELEMENTARY SCHOOL
1020 North Union Boulevard — opened 1907.
Named for: William Clark, one of the leaders of the Lewis and Clark expedition; appointed by President Jefferson as Indian Agent in St. Louis and later Governor of the Missouri territory.

4 FREMONT ELEMENTARY SCHOOL
2840 Wisconsin Avenue — opened 1897.
Named for: General John C. Fremont, explorer and soldier in Mexican-American War; commanded St. Louis headquarters of military government during the Civil War.

5 LACLEDE ELEMENTARY SCHOOL
5821 Kennerly — opened 1914.
Named for: Pierre Laclede, co-founder of St. Louis.

6 MARQUETTE ELEMENTARY SCHOOL
4015 McPherson — opened 1894.
Named for: Jacques Marquette; explored
the Mississippi River with Joliet.

7 MITCHELL ELEMENTARY SCHOOL
955 Arcade Avenue — opened 1964.
Named for: Joseph and William Mitchell,
founders and publishers of The St. Louis
Argus; crusaders for better education for
Negroes; active in Pine Street YMCA,
YWCA, NAACP, and Urban League.

8 SHEPARD ELEMENTARY SCHOOL
3450 Wisconsin Avenue — opened 1905.
Named for: Elihu H. Shepard, founder of
Missouri Historical Society; formed first
public school committee to organize Public
School System.

9 WINDSOR ELEMENTARY SCHOOL
4092 Robert Avenue — opened 1952.
Named for: Adelaide M. Windsor, a
founder of Child Conservation Conference
of St. Louis.

Public School Superintendents

1 HARRIS TEACHERS COLLEGE
3026 Laclede Avenue — opened 1927.
Named for: William Torrey Harris, superintendent of schools, 1867-1880.

2 SOLDAN HIGH SCHOOL
918 N. Union — opened 1909.
Named for: F. Louis Soldan, superintendent
of schools, 1895-1908.

3 BLEWETT ELEMENTARY SCHOOL
1927 Cass Avenue — opened 1956.
Named for: Dr. Ben Blewett, superintendent
of schools, 1908-1917; established Jessie
Parsons Blewett Fund for the relief of
teachers and for professional training.

4 DIVOLL ELEMENTARY SCHOOL
2918 Dayton Street — opened 1872.
Named for: Ira Divoll, founder of public
library system; superintendent of schools,
1859-1867.

5 LONG ELEMENTARY SCHOOL
5028 Morganford Road — opened 1922.
Named for: Edward Long, superintendent of
schools, 1880-1895.

6 MADDOX ELEMENTARY SCHOOL
6138 Virginia Avenue — opened 1911.
Named for: John H. Maddox, superintendent of instruction, 1921-1929.

Medical Men

1 BEAUMONT HIGH SCHOOL
3836 Natural Bridge — opened 1926.
Named for: William Beaumont, surgeon,
scientist, and author of book on digestion;
assigned to St. Louis Arsenal as surgeon
and medical officer.

2 CURTIS ELEMENTARY SCHOOL
2824 Madison Street — opened 1894.
Named for: Thomas A. and William P.
Curtis, brothers; St. Louis pioneer Negro
dentist and physician.

3 HODGEN ELEMENTARY SCHOOL
2748 Henrietta Street — opened 1884.
Named for: J. T. Hodgen, physician; nationally known as Surgeon General of the Western Sanitary Commission.

Educators

1 VASHON HIGH SCHOOL
3405 Bell — opened 1931.
Named for: George B. and John Vashon,
outstanding Negro educators; provided 75
years of consecutive leadership in education
both locally and nationally.

2 COLE ELEMENTARY SCHOOL
3935 Enright — opened 1931.
Named for: Richard H. Cole, public school
teacher; principal at the Simmons School
for fifty years.

3 ELIOT ELEMENTARY SCHOOL
4242 Grove Street — opened 1898.
Named for: William Greenleaf Eliot, secretary and president of the school board; founded Washington University; first Unitarian minister west of the Mississippi.

4 FANNING ELEMENTARY SCHOOL
3417 Grace Avenue — opened 1907.
Named for: Mrs. Rose Wright Fanning, teacher for forty-seven years and principal of Pestalozzi School.

5 FROEBEL ELEMENTARY SCHOOL
3709 Nebraska — opened 1895.
Named for: Friedrich Wilhelm August Froebel, originator of the Kindergarten.

6 HERZOG ELEMENTARY SCHOOL
5831 Pamplin — opened 1936.
Named for: Peter Herzog, teacher and principal for fifty years at the Blair School.

7 HOWARD ELEMENTARY SCHOOL
2333 Benton Street — opened 1902.
Named for: Professor Charles L. Howard, former principal of the Columbia School.

8 MANN ELEMENTARY SCHOOL
4047 Juniata — opened 1901.
Named for: Horace Mann, father of the American public school system; native of Massachusetts.

9 SIMMONS ELEMENTARY SCHOOL
4318 St. Louis Avenue — opened 1898.
Named for: William J. Simmons, St. Louis Baptist clergyman and educator.

10 WARING ELEMENTARY SCHOOL
25 South Compton Avenue — opened 1940.
Named for: Oscar Minor Waring, Greek and Latin scholar; first Negro principal of Sumner High School (1879).

11 WILLIAMS ELEMENTARY SCHOOL
3955 St. Ferdinand — opened 1964.
Named for: Frank L. Williams, principal Sumner High School (1908-1928); curator Lincoln University; active in YMCA work.

12 WOODWARD ELEMENTARY SCHOOL
725 Bellerive Boulevard — opened 1921.
Named for: Calvin Woodward, developed system of manual training used all over United States; Dean at Washington University; Board of Education member.

13 WYMAN ELEMENTARY SCHOOL
1547 South Theresa — opened 1901.
Named for: Edward Wyman, educator and founder of several schools; Director of St. Louis Public Schools and Curator of the University of Missouri.

Business Men/Philanthropists

1 O'FALLON TECHNICAL HIGH SCHOOL
5101 Northrup — opened 1956.
Named for: Colonel John O'Fallon, promoter of early railroad companies; financier; made large gifts to local universities.

2 AMES ELEMENTARY SCHOOL
2900 Hadley — opened 1956.
Named for: Henry Ames, St. Louis meat packer and hotel owner.

3 BUDER ELEMENTARY SCHOOL
5319 Lansdowne Avenue — opened 1920.
Named for: Mrs. Susan R. Buder, St. Louis jewelry store owner.

4 BUSCH ELEMENTARY SCHOOL
5910 Clifton — opened 1953
Named for: Adolphus Busch, St. Louis brewery owner and philanthropist.

5 CUPPLES ELEMENTARY SCHOOL
4908 Cote Brilliante — opened 1917.
Named for: Samuel Cupples, St. Louis wooden ware merchant; civic leader; donated large sums to Washington University.

6 DOZIER ELEMENTARY SCHOOL
5749 Maple — opened 1887.
Named for: James Dozier, St. Louis steamboat and bakery owner.

7 FORD ELEMENTARY SCHOOL
1383 Clara Avenue — opened 1964.
Named for: Henry and Edsel Ford, automobile manufacturers; established Ford Foundation.

8 GUNDLACH ELEMENTARY SCHOOL
2931 Arlington — opened 1931.
Named for: John H. Gundlach, St. Louis
real estate agent and worker for public improvements.

9 KENNARD ELEMENTARY SCHOOL
5031 Potomac Street — opened 1930.
Named for: Samuel M. Kennard, St. Louis
businessman.

10 MALLINCKRODT ELEMENTARY
SCHOOL
6020 Pernod — opened 1940.
Named for: Edward Mallinckrodt, native St.
Louis chemist and philanthropist.

11 MASON ELEMENTARY SCHOOL
6031 Southwest — opened 1919.
Named for: Isaac Mason, businessman,
Sheriff and Auditor of City of St. Louis.

12 MULLANPHY ELEMENTARY SCHOOL
4221 Shaw Boulevard — opened 1914.
Named for: Bryan Mullanphy, judge and
Mayor of St. Louis, and founder of Travelers
Aid Society.

13 PEABODY ELEMENTARY SCHOOL
1224 South Fourteenth Street —
opened 1957.
Named for: George Peabody, St. Louis
philanthropist and educator.

14 ROE ELEMENTARY SCHOOL
1921 Prather — opened 1922.
Named for: John Roe, steamboat captain,
meat packer, and contributor to Eads Bridge
construction.

15 SCULLIN ELEMENTARY SCHOOL
4160 North Kingshighway — opened 1928.
Named for: John Scullin, founder of St.
Louis steel company and bank director.

16 SHAW ELEMENTARY SCHOOL
5329 Columbia — opened 1907.
Named for: Henry Shaw, hardware merchant and founder of the Missouri Botanical
Garden (Shaw's Garden).

17 SCRUGGS ELEMENTARY SCHOOL
4611 South Grand Boulevard —
opened 1917.
Named for: Richard M. Scruggs, St. Louis
dry goods merchant; founder of Scruggs-
Vandervoort-Barney; director of Mercantile
Library Association.

18 STIX ELEMENTARY SCHOOL
226 South Euclid — opened 1922.
Named for: William Stix, dry goods merchant and founder of Rice-Stix Dry Goods
Company in St. Louis.

19 WADE ELEMENTARY SCHOOL
2030 South Vandeventer — opened 1930.
Named for: Festus Wade, president of the
Mercantile Trust Company and a St. Louis
real estate company.

20 WALBRIDGE ELEMENTARY SCHOOL
5000 Davison Avenue — opened 1922.
Named for: Cyrus P. Walbridge, St. Louis
drug company president and Mayor of
St. Louis.

21 WILKINSON ELEMENTARY SCHOOL
7212 Arsenal Street — opened 1927.
Named for: Melville Wilkinson, St. Louis
merchant, president of Scruggs.

Scientists

1 BANNEKER ELEMENTARY SCHOOL
2840 Lucas — opened 1932.
Named for: Benjamin Banneker, Negro
astronomer, mathematician, and one of the
architects who laid out the city of Washington, D. C.

2 CARVER ELEMENTARY SCHOOL
3325 Bell Avenue — opened 1882.
Named for: Dr. George Washington Carver,
scientist who went from slavery to college
professor; made many new products from
the peanut.

3 HUMBOLDT ELEMENTARY SCHOOL
2516 South Ninth Street — opened 1908.
Named for: Alexander Humboldt, scientist
and explorer.

4 TURNER MIDDLE SCHOOL
4235 W. Kennerly — opened 1925 and
2615 Pendleton — opened 1938.
Named for: Dr. Charles Henry Turner,
early Sumner High School faculty member;
famed for research on behavior using ants
and bees.

For Land Grants or Free Schools

1 BATES ELEMENTARY SCHOOL
1912 North Prairie — opened 1918.
Named for: Edward Bates, early St. Louis school director and lawyer; member of President Lincoln's cabinet.

2 CARR ELEMENTARY SCHOOL
1421 Carr Street — opened 1908.
Named for: William Carr, member of first Board of Education; helped to secure land grants; lawyer and judge.

3 HEMPSTEAD ELEMENTARY SCHOOL
5872 Minerva — opened 1907.
Named for: Edward Hempstead, member of first St. Louis School Board; Congressman, advocate of Federal land grants, speaker of the Missouri House of Representatives.

4 RIDDICK ELEMENTARY SCHOOL
4136 Evans — opened 1870.
Named for: Thomas Fiveash Riddick; made dramatic ride to Washington, D. C. to obtain land grant for free schools in St. Louis.

Writers

1 DUMAS ELEMENTARY SCHOOL
1409 North Fifteenth Street — opened 1870.
Named for: Alexander Dumas, French romantic novelist, author of such works as The Count of Monte Cristo and The Three Musketeers.

2 DUNBAR ELEMENTARY SCHOOL
1415 Garrison Avenue — opened 1912.
Named for: Paul Laurence Dunbar, Negro poet and writer distinguished for his collections of prose and poetry.

3 EMERSON ELEMENTARY SCHOOL
5415 Page Boulevard — opened 1901.
Named for: Ralph Waldo Emerson, American essayist, lecturer, and poet.

4 FIELD ELEMENTARY SCHOOL
4466 Olive Street — opened 1900.
Named for: Eugene Field, St. Louis born poet; author of such poems as Little Boy Blue and Gingham Dog and Calico Cat.

5 IRVING ELEMENTARY SCHOOL
3829 North Twenty-fifth Street — opened 1871.
Named for: Washington Irving, historian, novelist, essayist; wrote Rip Van Winkle.

6 LONGFELLOW ELEMENTARY SCHOOL
6593 Smiley Avenue — opened 1891.
Named for: Henry Wadsworth Longfellow, famous American poet and author of Hiawatha.

7 LOWELL ELEMENTARY SCHOOL
1409 Linton Avenue — opened 1926.
Named for: James Russell Lowell, American poet.

8 MARK TWAIN ELEMENTARY SCHOOL
5316 Ruskin Avenue — opened 1911.
Named for: Mark Twain (Samuel Clemens), American writer, humorist, and steamboat pilot.

9 WHEATLEY ELEMENTARY SCHOOL
4239 Papin Street — opened 1895.
Named for: Phyllis Wheatley, former slave who wrote poetry; second woman in the United States to have her works published.

Ministers

1 COOK ELEMENTARY SCHOOL
5935 Horton Place — opened 1964.
Named for: The Rev. James Cook, pastor of Antioch Baptist Church; Executive Secretary of the Pine Street YMCA; and known for his work with Negro youth.

2 STEVENS ELEMENTARY SCHOOL
1033 Whittier — opened 1964.
Named for: The Rev. George E. Stevens, pastor of Central Baptist Church; crusader for integrated schools; worked for good government; able leader in community activities; known as the "teachers' pastor."

Other Names

1 CENTRAL HIGH SCHOOL
3616 North Garrison — Erected 1904.
Central High School was opened February 11, 1853, and is now in the building formerly known as Yeatman High School, which was named after James Yeatman, president of the Western Sanitary Commission.

2 NORTHWEST HIGH SCHOOL
5140 Riverview Boulevard — opened 1964.
Named for its location.

3 SOUTHWEST HIGH SCHOOL
3125 South Kingshighway Boulevard — opened 1937.
Named for its location.

4 ARLINGTON ELEMENTARY SCHOOL
1617 Burd Avenue — opened 1899.
Named for the district in which it is situated, which was named for Arlington, Virginia.

5 ASHLAND ELEMENTARY SCHOOL
3921 North Newstead Avenue — opened 1909.
Named for: Ashland County, Kentucky, the home of Henry Clay. Clay once owned the land on which this school stands.

6 BADEN ELEMENTARY SCHOOL
8724 Halls Ferry Road — opened 1907.
Named for: Baden, Germany, city from which many of the early inhabitants came.

7 BRYAN HILL ELEMENTARY SCHOOL
2128 Gano Avenue — opened 1912.
Named for district owned by Dr. John Gano Bryan.

8 CARONDELET ELEMENTARY SCHOOL
8221 Minnesota Avenue — opened 1871.
Named for former city of Carondelet which got its name from Don Francisco Hector Luis el Baron de Carondelet, former Spanish Governor of Louisiana at New Orleans.

9 COLUMBIA ELEMENTARY SCHOOL
3120 St. Louis Avenue — opened 1929.
Named for: Columbia, a poetic name often given the United States.

10 COTE BRILLIANTE ELEMENTARY SCHOOL
2616 Cora Avenue — opened 1904.
Named for district or subdivision called "cote brilliante," after an Indian mound which was once in the neighborhood.

11 ENRIGHT MIDDLE SCHOOL
5351 Enright — erected 1905.
Named for the street which was named to honor Thomas Enright, one of the first soldiers to die in World War I.

12 GARDENVILLE ELEMENTARY SCHOOL
6651 Gravois Avenue — opened 1907.
Named for neighborhood location which was once occupied by market gardeners.

13 LINDENWOOD ELEMENTARY SCHOOL
3815 McCausland Avenue — opened 1929.
Named for school district which at one time was covered with linden trees.

14 MERAMEC ELEMENTARY SCHOOL
2745 Meramec Street — opened 1910.
Named for street on which it is located. Meramec is an Indian word meaning catfish.

15 MOUNT PLEASANT ELEMENTARY SCHOOL
4528 Nebraska — opened 1900.
Named for district and subdivision in south St. Louis where school is located.

16 OAK HILL ELEMENTARY SCHOOL
4300 Morganford Road — opened 1907.
Named for country home of Russell family, owners of extensive land in the neighborhood.

17 NOTTINGHAM ELEMENTARY SCHOOL
4915 Donovan Avenue — opened 1953.
Named for subdivision in which the streets were given English names.

18 ROCK SPRINGS ELEMENTARY SCHOOL
3974 Sarpy Avenue — opened 1899.
Named for school district which once had a rock spring.

19 SHENANDOAH ELEMENTARY SCHOOL
3412 Shenandoah Avenue — opened 1926.
Named for the street which was named for the Shenandoah River in Virginia. All of the east and west streets in the neighborhood are named for rivers.

20 WALNUT PARK ELEMENTARY SCHOOL
5814 Thekla — opened 1908.
Named for subdivision in which the school is located.

21 WELLS ELEMENTARY SCHOOL
5234 Wells Avenue — Erected 1928.
Named for the street. The street was named for Erastus Wells, first president of Street Railway Company in St. Louis; elected to Congress.

Selected References

1. Ames, Merlin and Lange, Dena. *St. Louis, Child of the River — Parent of the West*, Webster Publishing Company, 1939.

2. Conrad, Howard and Hyde, William. *Encyclopedia of the History of St. Louis*, Four vol., New York, 1899.

3. Davis, Julia. *Collection of Negro History*, St. Louis Public Library.

4. Gill, McCune. *The St. Louis Story*, St. Louis Historical Record Assn., 1952.

5. Kirschten, Ernest. *Catfish and Crystal*, New York, Doubleday and Co., Inc., 1960.

6. Quigley, Martin. *St. Louis — The First 200 Years*, St. Louis, 1964.

7. Scharf, J. Thomas. *History of St. Louis City and County*, Philadelphia, Louis H. Everts and Co., 1883.

8. Seifert, Shirley. *The Key to St. Louis*, New York, J. B. Lippincott Co., 1963.

9. Shoemaker, Floyd. *Missouri's Hall of Fame*, Columbia, Missouri, The Missouri Book Co., 1923.

10. Stadler, Frances. *St. Louis — From Laclede to Land Clearance*, St. Louis, 1962.

11. Stevens, Walter. *St. Louis — The Fourth City*, St. Louis, S. J. Clarke Publishing Co., 1909.

12. Young, N. B. *Your St. Louis and Mine*, St. Louis, 1937.

Picture Credits

ANHEUSER-BUSCH, INC., *174, 175*

OSCAR BERNINGHAUS, *Painting, 4*

WALTER BLACKWELL, *Drawing, 32*

MRS. BENJAMIN BUMBRY, *149*

CITY HALL COLLECTION, *iv, 3*

CAMPBELL HOUSE, *38*

MRS. LEWIS DAMMERT, *147*

DORRILL PHOTOGRAPHIC CO., *27*

TED FOX, *Drawings, 89, 118-120*

GLOBE-DEMOCRAT, *i, 49, 80, 140, 142*

GERTRUDE HOFFSTEN, *Maps, 1, 3, 9, 15*

JEFFERSON NATIONAL EXPANSION MEMORIAL, *8, 13, 29*

JULIUS JOHNSON, *Drawings, 138*

OTTO KEISKER, *Drawings, 180-185*

ART KIRCHOFF, *Drawings, xii, 98, 106*

LINDBERGH, *We, 90*

MISSOURI HISTORICAL SOCIETY, *Cover and End Papers, ii, 5, 14, 16, 17, 19, 22, 26, 28, 32, 34, 35, 37, 41-48, 52, 65, 68, 70, 74, 75, 77, 78, 81, 84, 86, 92, 100, 102, 104, 109, 113, 114, 122, 124, 128, 130, 137, 159, 160, 163-166, 179*

MISSOURI STATE CAPITAL, *65, 76, 81*

McDONNELL AIRCRAFT CORPORATION, *94-97*

MONSANTO CHEMICAL COMPANY, *170-173*

JEROME NENNINGER, *Drawing, 148*

ERIC P. NEWMAN NUMISMATIC EDUCATIONAL SOCIETY, *7, 72, 85*

OLD CATHEDRAL, *20, 21*

MARGARET POETKER, *10, 110, 111*

POST-DISPATCH, *vi, 53, 89, 93, 114, 115, 156, 157, 161, 167*

J. G. PRINCELL, *Photographs, 39, 68, 82, 83, 88, 105, 134, 135, 162, 168*

MRS. DOROTHY QUEST, *Painting of Laclede, 6*

ST. LOUIS ARGUS, *168, 169*

ST. LOUIS ART MUSEUM, *36, 153-155*

ST. LOUIS CHAMBER OF COMMERCE, *viii, 22, 26, 111, 139*

ST. LOUIS MEDICAL SOCIETY, *33*

ST. LOUIS MUNICIPAL OPERA ASSOCIATION, *134*

ST. LOUIS SYMPHONY SOCIETY, *144, 146*

ST. LOUIS ZOOLOGICAL GARDENS, *131, 132*

SCHARF, *History of St. Louis, 103*

SCOTTISH RITE CATHEDRAL HISTORY, *101*

WABASH RAILROAD, *81*

MICHAEL WEAVER, *Photographs, x, 12, 26, 30, 40*

HERB WEITMAN, *Photographs, 71, 150*

Index